Symbolic Interactionism

A Social Structural Version

The Benjamin/Cummings
SERIES IN CONTEMPORARY SOCIOLOGY

General editor: James F. Short, Jr.

Symbolic Interactionism

A Social Structural Version

SHELDON STRYKER

Department of Sociology
Indiana University

The Benjamin/Cummings Publishing Company
Menlo Park, California • Reading, Massachusetts
London • Amsterdam • Don Mills, Ontario • Sydney

Copyright © 1980 by the Benjamin/Cummings
Publishing Company, Inc. Philippines copyright
1980 by the Benjamin/Cummings Publishing
Company, Inc.

Library of Congress Cataloging in Publication Data

Stryker, Sheldon.
    Symbolic interactionism.

    (The Benjamin/Cummings series in contemporary
sociology
    Includes index.
    1. Symbolic interactionism. I. Title. II. Series:
Benjamin/Cummings series in contemporary sociology.
HM24.S787   301.11   79-24439
ISBN 0-8053-9154-1

ABCDEFGHIJ-AL—83210

The Benjamin/Cummings Publishing Company, Inc.
2727 Sand Hill Road
Menlo Park, California 94025

For Alyce

Contents

Foreword

I am happy to provide this brief foreword to an important segment of the *Benjamin/Cummings Series in Contemporary Sociology*—a segment devoted to the systematic exposition and critique of major theoretical perspectives in the discipline.

This volume on *Symbolic Interactionism,* by Sheldon Stryker, combined with *Functionalism,* by Jonathan Turner, and the forthcoming *Conflict Theory,* by Austin Turk, form a "trilogy" on the three most important theoretical perspectives in sociology.

Each volume explores the historical roots as well as contemporary developments in a major theoretical orientation, appreciation as well as critique. Each will examine its subject as theory and as method in an effort to acquaint students with the important relationships between them in the sociological enterprise.

Here, as with all volumes in the *Benjamin/Cummings Series in Contemporary Sociology,* we solicit critique, rebuttal, and the challenge of disciplined inquiry so essential to the advancement of knowledge.

James F. Short, Jr.

Preface

This is a book that tries to develop a particular line of sociological theorizing—symbolic interactionism—by describing some of its history, delineating a personal version of it oriented to particular criteria of "good" sociological theory, and describing some variants of symbolic interactionist theory that are consonant with these criteria. It is a book that is addressed not so much to the past as to the future, to the directions that developments in symbolic interactionist theory and research ought to take to realize its potential as sound and productive sociological theory.

As such, the book does not hold itself responsible for a "full" treatment of all that has been labelled, or could be labelled, symbolic interactionist; it does not pretend to comprehensiveness in this respect. With one exception, deemed necessary to enable the student to understand why the characteristic emphases in the variants of symbolic interactionism are reviewed, this text omits from consideration a whole wing of symbolic interactionist writers. This very wing with which the position is popularly identified is omitted on the grounds that its purposes and intents are different from those pursued in the book. My reading of the work of those "located" in this wing is that their views of science, theory, and social structure are very different from those underlying my treatment of symbolic interactionism. Thus, many persons of strong and justifiable reputation identified with symbolic interactionism have not been treated.

Further, the book does not concern itself with substantive applications of symbolic interactionist theorizing. Its premise is that the central themes of that theorizing can be described and analyzed without extending its coverage to the use of the approach in dealing with such substantive topics as deviance and collective behavior. True, the central themes would have to be extended or specified beyond their treatment here to be completely useful in such applications; but the extension and specification were taken to be beyond the scope of the present effort.

The idea for this book originated with Larry Wilson, Sponsoring Editor for the Benjamin/Cummings Publishing Company. However much of the result may mutilate Larry's original idea, I am grateful to him. I am also grateful to a number of persons who read the manuscript and commented on it, or discussed with me one or another point contained in it: Carl Backman, Leonard Beeghley, Peter Burke, Thomas Gieryn, Morris Rosenberg, James Short, and Ralph Turner. No one other than myself is responsible for any flaws that remain.

Sheldon Stryker

Introduction

Some Orienting Remarks

Symbolic interactionism has been regarded both as a general framework for the analysis of society,[1] and as a relatively specialized social psychological theory addressed primarily to problems of socialization.[2] It is in the former context that it will be presented, discussed and evaluated in this volume. As defined and delimited by many of its most vigorous and partisan proponents, symbolic interactionism is neither a well formulated theory nor an adequate framework for dealing with the full range of intellectual problems sociologists choose to focus upon. In particular, it is suggested that in order to be satisfactory, the framework must incorporate concepts that more adequately refer to social structure than is the case in some versions of the theory. Versions of the framework which seek to do this will be presented.

Apart from inadequately dealing with the facts of social structure, some versions of symbolic interactionism seem to deny the possibility of research on human social behavior within the boundaries of science, as science is conventionally understood. Another major argument is that the dis-

---

[1]Herbert Blumer, *Symbolic Interactionism: Perspective and Method* (Englewood Cliffs, N.J.: Prentice Hall, 1969).

[2]Sheldon Stryker, "The Interactional and Situational Approaches," in Harold Christensen, ed., *Handbook of Marriage and the Family* (Chicago: Rand McNally, 1964), pp. 125-169.

1

sociation of symbolic interactionism from conventional science is neither warranted nor wise.

As these orienting remarks are intended to suggest, there are quite different ideas to which the label "symbolic interactionism" may be said to apply. On the other hand, there is a core of ideas which unites different versions whatever their variation on other accounts. While this core is spelled out in later chapters, it may be well to note in a preliminary way that symbolic interactionists are united in their view that both society and person are abstractions from ongoing social interaction, that "selves" and "society" have no reality apart from one another or from the interpersonal interactions from which they derive, and that both self and society are essential to an understanding of social interaction. They are united, as well, by a basic methodological dictum:[3] the point of view of the participants in social interaction must enter decisively into satisfactory accounts or explanations of that interaction. The methodological directive contained in this dictum follows directly from W. I. Thomas' assertion, perhaps the most quoted phrase in the literature of symbolic interactionism: "If men define situations as real, they are real in their consequences."[4]

The unity of and the variation within symbolic interactionism is the subject matter of this book, which seeks not only to describe but to appraise. But before embarking on further elaboration, it may help the reader to have an overview of the volume as a whole.

An Overview of Chapter Content

This initial chapter provides an orientation to the book. It summarizes the major arguments, and specifies the premises underlying the arguments and the manner in which they are made. These premises—about the nature of theory, the nature of science, and the "fit" of various versions of symbolic interactionism to the premises about theory and science—structure the way in which symbolic interactionism is described and appraised. It is, therefore,

---

[3]Some very different implications are drawn from this dictum, of a type hinted at by a prior comment on symbolic interactionism and conventional science.

[4]William I. Thomas and Dorothy S. Thomas, *The Child in America* (New York: Knopf, 1928), p. 572.

helpful for the reader to keep them in mind as the remainder of the book is read.

A sense that various versions of symbolic interactionism are differentially attuned to and successful in incorporating social structural concepts, and a judgment that some versions are neither sympathetic to nor consistent with one or another of my premises about the nature of theory and of science, have led to decisions restricting the coverage of this work. In particular, to readers at all aware of what has been done under the rubric of symbolic interactionism, the fact that Chapter 4 does not review the ideas of such persons as Anselm Strauss, Howard Becker, Erving Goffman, Gregory Stone, Tamotsu Shibutani, Norman Denzin—as well as others—may come as something of a shock and be seen as an indicator of irresponsibility. The ommission of such persons, whose contributions would have to be recognized by any study pretending to comprehensive coverage of symbolic interactionism, underscores my very different intent in the present context: the pursuit of a symbolic interactionism that is at once true to the basic vision of the perspective; sensitive to the realities of social structure as these constrain and facilitate social behavior; cognizant of the limitations of any single perspective; operative within the framework of science in seeking general, empirically-based and supported explanations; and nonexclusionary in its view of proper methods of doing sociology.

Maines[5] has argued that the characterization of the wing of symbolic interactionism largely ommitted in this book as not attuned to social structure is faulty. He makes the case that social organizational considerations are more organic to Herbert Blumer's work than is commonly believed; and he develops the thesis, using in particular Anselm Strauss' writings, that the concept of negotiated order and the idea that negotiations take place in context whose features affect the ongoing negotiations evidence the successful incorporation of structural elements into symbolic interactionism. There is certainly some validity in Maines' argument. In my judgment, however, the analytic possibilities of "negoti-

---

[5]David R. Maines, "Social Organization and Social Structure in Symbolic Interactionist Thought," in Alex Inkeles, James Coleman, and Neil Smelser, eds., *Annual Review of Sociology* (Palo Alto, Calif.: Annual Reviews Inc., 1977), pp. 235-259.

ated order" are too limited, and the way in which these possibilities are developed too unsystematic, to merit serious consideration as an alternative to the kind of social structural conceptualization offered in Chapters 3 and 4.

There is another coverage "gap" in the chapters that follow. The basic ideas of symbolic interactionist thinking have been used to deal with a wide variety of substantive topics, from individual behavior and social interaction in particular contexts such as the family, to deviance and collective behavior and beyond. Indeed, the perspective is most frequently seen in application in studies of family relationships, of deviance, and of collective behavior. There is very little in the chapters to follow that directly reflects such substantive concerns, although what is said is certainly germane. Again, it is a matter of intent. A comprehensive text covering all of symbolic interactionism would certainly have to describe such applications. A book that fails to do so runs the risk of incompletely presenting the framework. Given that work in deviance and in collective behavior also take as an important issue the linkage of social structure to social interaction and individual behavior, there is also the risk of being misleading with respect to the adequacy (or inadequacy) of particular versions of symbolic interactionism in dealing with that central issue. I have chosen to run those risks in order to concentrate on what I take to be the major themes of the framework, and these can be presented without entering specialized domains of application.

Chapter 2 traces the background of symbolic interactionism, beginning with the Scottish moral philosophers of the 18th century—especially David Hume, Adam Smith and Adam Fergusen— and moves to the American pragmatic philosophers William James, John Dewey and George Herbert Mead. Discussed as part of this stream of development, and important to it, are the psychologist James Mark Baldwin and the sociologists Charles Horton Cooley and William Isaac Thomas. Precisely because of the book's argument that some variants of symbolic interactionism fail to treat social structure adequately, a brief discussion of some precursors— Georg Simmel, Max Weber, and Ralph Linton—of so-called role theory is included in this historical chapter. It is the melding of concepts and ideas of role theory into concepts and ideas developed by Mead et al. that permits some variants of symbolic interactionism to be regarded as a reasonably suitable framework for the analysis of sociological as well as social psychological questions.

It is this melding of concepts and ideas that is presented in Chapter 3—my current statement of symbolic interactionism. Many will object to this statement as departing significantly and in principle from what they understand by symbolic interactionism. But if one does not regard some extant version of the theoretical framework as revealed or established Truth, then it must be open to change. And if one holds as criteria for seeking to change the framework, its adequacy in scientific terms and its responsibility to sociological—i.e., social-structural—issues, then the additions through role theory make sense and can be justified. In any event, this chapter does in fact present as one version of symbolic interactionism a hybrid characterization drawing on Simmel, Weber, Linton (and others), as well as James, Thomas, Cooley, Mead (and others).

Chapter 4 examines variants among symbolic interactionists. Historically, two "opposing" schools of symbolic interactionism have been defined, the first identified with the University of Chicago and Herbert Blumer, the second with the University of Iowa and Manfred Kuhn. Blumer's distinctive emphases are examined first[6] and then attention is turned to Kuhn. In addition, the work of a number of contemporary symbolic interactionists, none of whom is easily categorized as belonging with either Blumer or Kuhn, is briefly reviewed. Perhaps it is reasonable to label this group—I see myself within it—as "the independents,"

[6]Given the previous comments on omissions of persons identified as symbolic interactionists, the reader might well wonder why Blumer's work is reviewed. There are two reasons. Blumer is the intellectual godfather of the so-called Chicago School of symbolic interactionism, and one way of seeing the characteristic emphases of this wing of the framework is through his work. More relevant, however, is the fact that in considerable degree the characteristic emphases of the alternatives discussed through this book developed in response to Blumer. It is thus important to their understanding to have available the picture of Blumer's work.

My assertion of Blumer's role as intellectual godfather of the Chicago symbolic interactionists may well slight the influence of two eminent Chicago sociologists. Ralph Turner (personal communication) has suggested that Everett Hughes' significance in stimulating a more open and structurally-relevant symbolic interactionism is now being recognized, and that Hughes' influence may especially be seen in Anselm Strauss' work. I have long believed that the view of Erving Goffman as *sui generis* fails to understand the way in which his writing reflects W. I. Thomas.

meaning by that phrase both freedom from the traditional schools and internal variation. Particular attention is given to Ralph Turner and George McCall; Eugene Weinstein and Peter Burke are more briefly dealt with.

A critique of symbolic interactionism follows in Chapter 5 where a number of standard criticisms that have been levied against the position are reviewed. Specifying to which of the variants of the position particular critical judgments do and do not apply is attempted; the cogency and appropriateness of these judgments are assessed; and a concluding appraisal is offered.

Underlying Premises

In an interesting and controversial reading of the recent past, the present, and the future of sociological theory, Mullins[7] describes symbolic interaction theory as the "loyal opposition" to the dominant sociological paradigm of the 1950's and the 1960's: structural-functionalism. In so labelling symbolic interactionism, Mullins intends to assert its secondary position among the perspectives available for the study of social life. Beyond that, however, he clearly sees symbolic interaction theory as fighting a rear-guard action for its very survival and as destined to fail in that struggle. Its fate, as Mullins sees it, is to disappear while new sociological paradigms take center stage.

This volume is premised on the belief that Mullins is wrong, perhaps misled by a regional myopia that frequently has distorted the readings sociologists take of their discipline. Perhaps, too, he has been misled by a vision of change and succession in scientific theories that emphasizes revolutionary breaks rather than evolutionary developments or even dialectic processes resulting in eventual syntheses.

At any rate, there are reasons to hold the view that symbolic interaction theory—properly understood—has a viability and a vitality that promises continuing influence and long life albeit not a static content. The continuous flow of theoretical writing and research explicitly linked to this

[7]Nicholas C. Mullins, *Theories and Theory Groups in Contemporary American Sociology* (New York: Harper & Row, 1973).

theory, the even greater flow of work that bears the imprint of its essential ideas even when the linkage is not explicitly made, and the emergence of a Society for the Study of Symbolic Interaction, do not testify to the demise that Mullins predicts. The "loyal opposition" figure Mullins uses to characterize symbolic interaction theory may have been aptly chosen, but perhaps not for the reasons he chose it. The figure evolves from a political idiom, and is peculiarly appropriate for a view which likely depends more on one-time political dominance of central figures in the professional organization of sociologists and on where they became sociological citizens (i.e., trained in the field) than on a valid assessment of the dominance of theoretical ideas per se.

Whether Mullins is wrong and the alternative proposed in the foregoing is correct, however, is not what is important in the present context.[8] What is important is that the content of this book will have been affected by the views of its author. Therefore, understanding the assumptions that provide the meta-theoretical underpinnings for the rest of the volume is useful for the reader.

This book is not intended as a study in the history of ideas, nor is it meant to be an endeavor in the sociology of sociology. Thus, the fact it was written at all testifies to the initial and most important assumption being made: the central ideas of symbolic interactionism are both sound and fruitful within the framework of science. A second, related assumption, is that the quality of sociological ideas—their soundness, their fertility, and their appropriateness from the standpoint of a scientific enterprise—rather than the political dominance of those who hold ideas will ultimately determine whether the ideas will prevail or will fade from the scene. Certainly the label "symbolic interactionism" may eventually wind up in disuse; this is particularly likely

[8]My own assessment here may be too dependent on having been schooled in the midwest and having spent virtually all of my professional life in that region. In professional sociology, the midwest is both the traditional center of interactionist thinking, and the traditional source of resentment against the political hegemony of the "Eastern Establishment." There is another possible reading of the history of American symbolic interactionism, suggested by Ralph Turner (personal communication). Developing initially as the social scientific expression of political liberalism, it began to fade in prominence with the advent of a sociology as hard science view, began its re-emergence slowly during the ascendance of structure-functionalism, and then grew rapidly as an alternative to polarized functionalism and conflict theory.

if and when sociological terms are more rarely used as shib-
boleths and battle cries for social movements within sociology. Whether or not the label disappears, however, the ideas
may not, except in the sense that they no longer have limited, sectarian appeal but are basic to the orientation of the
discipline at large. In important measure, this has already
happened to central features of symbolic interactionism,
and it may be that the process will continue. In this ironic
sense, Mullins may be correct: by being absorbed into sociology at large, symbolic interactionism may disappear, may
—in other words—lose by winning!

On Theory and Frames of Reference

It should be noted that the language of the preceding paragraph is that of "central ideas" and not of "theory." This
choice of words reflects further assumptions, one being that
symbolic interactionism does not at this point constitute a
satisfactory sociological theory. Indeed, if the ideas of symbolic interactionism have been used as the basis for any
theory in a technical sense, it is with respect to a relatively
specialized set of problems largely having to do with socialization.

This judgment rests on a particular use of the term "theory"; in this usage, a set of logically related hypotheses specifying expected relationships among variables, based on
concepts describing selected aspects of the world and assumptions about the way it works, and open to falsification
through evidence drawn from the world.[9] In this respect, a
theory is obviously more than a set of concepts drawing
attention to particular aspects of the empirical world
thought to be of special import in the understanding of that
world; for the latter, the language of "frame of reference,"
"conceptual framework," or "perspective" is reserved. A
theory will incorporate the concepts provided by a frame of
reference, but the two do not refer to equivalent phenomena. With respect to the world of interest to the sociologist,
the judgment being expressed is that symbolic interactionism is a frame of reference or a perspective. It tells the
sociologist, for example, that the world as experienced by
those persons studied is of critical importance; it suggests

[9]Stryker, op. cit., pp. 125–127.

that if sociology is to make headway in understanding social order and social change, the sociologist must comprehend the meaning of facts of the environment, of social relationships, and of intra-psychic "forces" as these are provided meaning by the participants in interaction. In brief, it specifies what sociologists should be sensitive to in the infinite world available for observation, and it argues that what it directs attention to is important relative to other possible foci of attention.

But a frame of reference does not specify just what connections can be expected among those aspects of the world singled out for special attention: it tells us, by way of illustration, that "role" and "self" are likely to be significant variables in a problem of interest, but it does not tell us how "role" and "self" are connected or how they relate to whatever we may be researching. Nor does it necessarily claim (whatever the claims made by persons promoting a frame of reference) that what it focuses on is *all* that is of import; indeed, at least implicitly, by heightening our attention to specific parts of the empirical world, it announces that it cannot pay attention to every part of that world. A frame of reference, in short, must give short shrift to some potentially significant determinants of social behavior by the very act of directing attention to its special concerns. It must be so because, again, the empirical world is infinite; because aspects of that world are subject to an infinite variety of classificatory and conceptual schemes; and because the very nature of scientific explanation requires that the world be simplified in some ways in order to be studied at all.

Thus, any given frame of reference leaves open the question of whether alternative perspectives can suggest other variables necessary to understanding the social world; and it leaves open the question of the ways in which these other variables, suggested by alternative perspectives, may fit its own emphases. Any given frame of reference, to make the point in another way, is not exclusionary.

From the point of view being expressed, arguing that symbolic interactionism is a frame of reference implies that within social psychology, it can legitimately accept lessons to be learned from work done from an exchange framework, or from an operant conditioning framework. Within sociology, it can accept the lessons available from a structural-functional, conflict, or some other alternative perspective.

It is necessary to return to one element in the view of theory with which this discussion began, namely, that which defined theory as open to falsification. Implied here is the readiness to reject theoretically-derived hypotheses on evidential grounds, and the consequent readiness to reject as untenable, a theory from which the hypotheses were drawn. While one could not reject a frame of reference on evidential grounds, one could reject or alter that framework on grounds that it failed to yield theory which did in fact stand the test of evidence. Readiness to reject or reformulate in the face of evidence is a hallmark of the scientific attitude. And that comment leads to another set of premises on the basis of which the next chapters are developed.

On Science

Thus far, attention has been centered on the ideas of "theory" and of "frame of reference," and on the underlying premises of these ideas incorporated in subsequent chapters of this book. It is time to turn briefly[10] to premises with respect to the nature of the scientific enterprise.

Part of what needs to be said is implied in the prior discussion. If any frame of reference omits or slights potential variables of importance in explaining some behavior, it is impossible to achieve—within the limits of a theory working with a finite set of concepts provided by the frame of reference—a total explanation of that behavior. Sociologists work with a set of social variables and seek to explain human behavior with those variables; they do not include in their theories physiological, chemical, or physical variables that may affect behavior. Thus any sociological explanation will be partial and incomplete.

There are views of science which argue that the world must be "deterministic" if science is to exist.[11] All behavior

---

[10]Necessarily so. This is not the place to fully develop and seek to justify a philosophy of science.

[11]So, for example, see Kenneth J. Gergen, "Social Psychology as History," *Journal of Personality and Social Psychology*, 26 (June, 1973):309–320, for an expression of this point of view in the context of social psychology. And see Sheldon Stryker, "Developments in the 'Two Social Psychologies': Toward an Appreciation of Mutual Relevance," *Sociometry*, 40 (June, 1977):145–160, for a partial rebuttal.

must be caused, and it must be possible to explicate a complete set of causes sufficient to account for every case without exception of some behavior. However, another view is available. In this alternative view, there is no need to assume a completely deterministic universe to justify science. Rather, one need only assume that there is some regularity in the behavior one is interested in; and the task of a science becomes to describe and explain that regularity insofar as it exists. A search for general "truth" does not require a completely deterministic universe.[12]

Similarly, and again given the view of theory as expressed as well as the view of science being developed, an adequate scientific explanation does not demand that every particular case fall into the pattern demanded by a generalized explanation of the class of cases under examination. There are a number of elements in this complex assertion that need to be expanded. The first is that science does indeed seek explanations of *classes* of events, or behaviors, and not particular events or behaviors. Obviously, no two events or behaviors are precisely alike if only in that they must occur in different space-time configurations. If two or more events or behaviors are to be placed in the same class in order to try to develop an explanation that holds for the class, some particularities of those events or behaviors must be ignored. Thus, science can never comprehend events or behaviors in their full complexity. And, it may be that some characteristic of the event or behavior that is omitted from consideration is critical for its explanation. Implied here is the further assertion that aspiring to an explanation that will hold for every concrete, complex event or behavior is unrealistic, however useful the aspiration may be from the standpoint of developing a set of work rules for science. Or, to make the point more positively, all scientific explanations are probabilistic in form.

While these assertions, it is arguable, hold for science in

[12]One of the major themes of theoretical work in a symbolic interactionist framework, strongly influenced as this has been by G. H. Mead, is that there is an indeterminacy of sorts in behavior, in the form of choice, self-direction, and self-control. The symbolic interactionist sees such choice, self-direction, and self-control as socially derived, that is, as rooted in social interaction. Moreover, to see behavior (in part or even totally) as the product of choice is certainly not to view behavior as random.

general, they are particularly true for a science which draws its data from the everyday world of social interaction. That everyday world is indeed extremely complex, the number and range of variables entering it being so great as to make every instance of interaction unique in some respects. Thus, the search for general patterns of social behavior and general explanations for those patterns observed will necessarily ignore that which may be idiosyncratic about some particular instances of interaction but nevertheless critical for how those instances develop. And thus, some instances will develop in ways contrary to the general run of cases and so prove to be exceptions from the point of view of the general explanation proferred. Again, the point is that this is in the nature of the sociological enterprise and does not in itself defeat the effort to work within the conventions of science.

Given the problem one is interested in studying, these conventions call for, among other things, achieving the greatest possible degree of control over observations. The form of control sought will certainly vary. Some problems —for example, seeking what it may be that affects the coalition behavior of persons in competitive situations—are amenable to experimental investigation in terms relatively close to the classical laboratory experiment. Other problems—for example, investigating the effects of income and education on the attainment of status—cannot be studied experimentally, but controlled observations may be achievable through statistical techniques of data manipulation. Still other problems—an example might be a study of the conditions affecting the occurence of wars between nations —may occur too infrequently to enable efficient statistical controls, but one can seek the advantages of controlled observations through the selection of appropriate historical cases. Whatever the problem, there will be some manner in which the ideal of controlled observations may be approximated; and the only rule that applies is that one must seek the best methods possible given the nature of the problem at hand. No method need be ruled out on *a priori* grounds. More to the immediate point, a premise of this account of symbolic interactionism is that there is no inherent contradiction between the methods of experimentation, mathematical or statistical analysis, historical analysis, or whatever, and the fundamental ideas of symbolic interactionism.

In the view of science being outlined here, the objective of sociology is to develop theoretical explanations of social behavior. It is not the "discovery" of immutable laws of social behavior, but the invention of theoretical accounts for such regularities in social behavior as may exist. The ongoing business of sociology as science is the test of alternative, theoretical accounts through controlled observational techniques. That business is conducted both inductively and deductively. That is, a research effort may begin with the intensive observation and examination of cases or instances of social behavior and move towards the development of a theory which serves to explain those instances; or it may begin with a theory from which hypotheses are logically derived and then move to cases or instances which are examined to see whether the hypotheses hold. Presumably, if experience is slight and theory only weakly developed, wisdom requires a heavily inductive procedure; on the other hand, where experience is considerable and theory well developed, one can work effectively in a deductive mode. The business of science requires both, for it (as is implied by the rejection of the discovery of immutable laws as the objective of science) is a never-ending process of moving from observations to possible explanations to observations *ad infinitum*.

The position just taken is not universally acceptable, to make the point mildly, among those who call themselves symbolic interactionists. For many, the ideas of symbolic interactionism are defined in *opposition to* such alternatives as behaviorism (in social psychology) or structural-functionalism (in sociology). For many such persons, symbolic interactionism is not one among a number of alternative perspectives; it is rather the Truth, and as such is not subject to challenge or change.

There are certain views which serve as "flags" in identifying those who take a dogmatic view of the ideas of symbolic interactionism, persons who tend to take stands not unlike members of a social movement. These include seeing humans as qualitatively different from other, nonhuman, animals, the focus being on symbolic interaction— and in particular language—as the differentiating feature;

an insistence that internal communication made possible by symbolic capabilities removes humans from the deterministic world that nonhumans inhabit; the urging of the distinctive character of social science based on a view of determinism as an essential of conventional science; a consequent rejection of conventional science; a correlative rejection of so-called hypothetical-deductive procedures and an insistence on a totally inductive stance; the assertion that "meaning" cannot be captured in numerical terms and the rejection of quantitative work for that reason; the reliance on direct observation or on sympathetic introspection (a la Cooley); and the denial of the validity, under any circumstances, of the experiment or the survey as a source of sociological data.

Indeed, the foregoing "flags" are precisely what the label "symbolic interactionism" is likely to conjure up in the minds of most social scientists even vaguely familiar with the label. It has been the burden of this section on theory and science to say: "It ain't necessarily so!"

2

The Background of Symbolic Interactionism

Introduction

The label, "symbolic interactionism," was invented by Herbert Blumer,[1] whose views are examined in detail in another chapter. The ideas signified by symbolic interactionism, however, have a much longer heritage. Blumer lists among the American scholars who have used this approach or contributed to its development: George Herbert Mead, John Dewey, William James, W. I. Thomas, Robert Redfield, and Louis Wirth.[2] The listing is instructive in at least two respects: it is headed by a set of pragmatic philosophers; and it includes a large representation of scholars connected with the University of Chicago. Both of these characteristics have played important roles in shaping the perspective, and help to account for the emphases given to symbolic interactionism in the work of Blumer and many others as well.

As distinguished as the list is, it could easily be expanded even within the same time frame (the late nineteenth century, early twentieth century) and the same geographic frame (the United States) that Blumer chose to use. If one goes beyond these frames of era and location, the candidates for a list of important contributors expands greatly.

[1]The term first appeared in Blumer's chapter in Emerson P. Schmitt, ed., *Man and Society* (New York: Prentice-Hall, 1937).
[2]Herbert Blumer, *Symbolic Interactionism: Perspective and Method* (Englewood Cliffs, N.J.: Prentice-Hall, 1969), p. 1.

We need not be concerned with developing an inclusive roster of significant historical figures in the background of symbolic interactionism; nor do we need to defend or rationalize the inclusion or exclusion of some particular figure. The relevance of history for present purposes is limited, and will not be met by name-dropping no matter how distinguished the names. It will be enough to trace briefly a major historical stream leading to contemporary versions of the theory, and an important tributary to that major stream. We do so for several reasons: (1) so students will be aware, even to a limited extent, that sociological ideas do not grow in a vacuum uninfluenced by modes of thought in philosophy, in other social sciences, or, indeed, in the full range of scientific and humane disciplines; (2) so students will come to understand that theoretical ideas are not to be identified with one or another contemporary proponent, or group of proponents, but have a life and a development of their own; (3) to emphasize what students often now do not see: that sociology does in fact develop, that is, the lines of thought comprising sociology grow through processes of challenge and response, of thinking through the logic of the lines themselves, and of confronting thought with evidence; (4) to better reveal problems inherent in one or another aspect of the line of thought with which we are concerned.

But limiting the task to tracing a major historical stream and tributary has a highly arbitrary quality. Where does one start and how deeply does one plumb? It has been said, with more than a little justice, that every aspect of western thought can be traced back to Aristotle.

The Scottish Moral Philosophers

We will not go back to Aristotle. Instead, we start with a set of Scottish moral philosophers. Gladys Bryson[3] has provided the rationale for this beginning: the 18th century saw the attempt to establish an empirical basis for the study of human beings and society, and it was this particular group of men—David Hume, Frances Hutcheson, Adam Smith, Adam Ferguson, and others—whose efforts in this direction

---

[3]Gladys Bryson, *Man and Society: The Scottish Inquiry of the Eighteenth Century* (Princeton, N.J.: Princeton University Press, 1945), p. 1.

influenced early American sociology and social psychology.[4] As we shall see, what these men had to say, while important to the development of sociology and social psychology in general, is of peculiar relevance to the development of symbolic interactionism.

The Scottish moral philosophers were empiricists. Less committed to metaphysics and more to the analysis of the business of living than the label "moral philosopher" might imply to a modern ear, they took philosophy to be (in Adam Smith's words) ". . . the science of the connecting principles of nature."[5] Or, as one of the group expressed it:

> The ultimate object of philosophical inquiry is the same which every man of plain understanding proposes to himself, when he remarks the events which fall under his observation, with a view to the future regulation of his conduct. The more knowledge of this kind we acquire, the better can we accommodate our plans to the established order of things, and avail ourselves of natural powers and agents for accomplishing our purposes.[6]

As a group, then, the Scottish moral philosophers were committed to empiricism and to induction; and they saw these as leading to useful knowledge. When they called for observation of man and his relationships, they were calling for the observation of their own everyday experience. They did not experiment; they did not manipulate and control; and verification was largely a matter of expanding their field of observation. Their forte was theorizing, and they theorized by referring their observations to organizing principles which were themselves taken for granted.

What, then, were these organizing principles? These were to be found in an understanding of human nature, by discovering through observation (largely introspective) what is most fundamental about the human mind. As reliance on introspection might suggest, the moralists disagreed among themselves about just what was in fact fundamental; they denied that men were motivated by rea-

---

[4]Ibid., Chapter 1. Bryson suggests that their influence was felt, in particular, by McDougall in social psychology and by Giddings and Small in sociology.

[5]Adam Smith, *Essays on Philosophical Subjects* (London, 1795), p.20. Quoted in Bryson, op. cit., p. 16.

[6]Dugald Stewart, *Collected Works,* Sir William Hamilton, ed., (Edinburgh, 1854–1860), Vol. II, p. 6. Quoted in Bryson, op. cit., p. 16.

son, but they saw the source of human action variously in sympathy, common sense, moral sense, belief, instinct, and habit, indeed in a full range of sentiments and sensations. Overriding this diversity, however, and much more significant from the point of view of an emergent symbolic interactionism, was a common conviction that while psychology as the science of man was basic to an understanding of society, psychology itself could not be comprehended without taking into account the facts of human association.

Bryson makes clear the implications of this last assertion when, in discussing the views of human nature held by the Scottish moral philosophers, she notes:

> They were far more interested in the life of men, the life of activity, than they were with the purely intellectual processes. They would not have opposed the statement popular with us that man is not born human, but becomes human by virtue of his societal life. And so we find in all their writings great attention to communication, sympathy, imitation, habit and convention, which take us, on mention of the words, into the realm of our associated life.[7]

When our contemporaries think of Adam Smith, they think of his role in shaping classical economic thought through his work on the wealth of nations. They are less prepared, if at all, to see Smith as a forerunner or anticipator of symbolic interaction theory. The following passage, again emphasizing the degree to which the human is dependent upon association with others for the very conception of self, could well have been written by Charles Horton Cooley and anticipates Cooley's conception of the looking glass self. Smith is discussing the consequences of isolation from communication with others:

> Bring him into society, and he is immediately provided with the mirror which he wanted before. It is placed in the countenance and behavior of those he lives with. This is the only looking glass by which we can, in some measure, with the eyes of other people, scrutinize the propriety of our own conduct.[8]

[7]Bryson, op. cit., pp. 146-147.
[8]Adam Smith, *Theory of Moral Sentiments* (London, 1759). Quoted in Bryson, op. cit., p. 161.

It is perhaps especially in discussions of sympathy that the Scottish moral philosophers anticipate the contemporary symbolic interactionist. Consider the views of David Hume. Humans are born into family units, and must maintain society by virtue of necessity, natural inclination, and habit. Weak and defective alone, it is society—initially, the family—that compensates for these deficiencies. Humans are neither unsocial nor antisocial; but in consequence of the ties between parents and children, and the fact of infancy, the interests of individual and community are increasingly tied together. There is a principle—sympathy— that operates in human beings and that develops fellow feeling and a concern for society as well as a sense of benefits to be expected from society. Sympathy is a psychological tendency to share the feelings of others, to obtain through communication other persons' sentiments and desires even when these differ greatly from our own. "No sooner any person approaches me, than he diffuses on me all his opinions, and draws along my judgment in a greater or lesser degree ... the minds of men are mirrors to one another."[9]

For Adam Smith, too, sympathy is a universal human trait, largely unlearned, which allows us to put ourselves in another's place and to see the world through that other person's eyes. It is not pity or compassion, but it permits us to participate in any emotion or experience of another. Sympathy is the ability human beings have to receive subtle and open communications from others; these communications alter who and what we are. It is through communicating with others that we first learn about ourselves; and we continuously change ourselves to win the approval of these others. Society becomes a vast network of interpersonal communication through which the participants are controlled by the approval and disapproval, the desires and the evaluations, of others. As Bryson says: "... in these discussions of Smith's—as in those of Hume— which prefigure so much of modern social psychology, there sometimes seems to be no individuals at all, so organic is the relation of person to person conceived to be."[10]

The same "organic" relationship of person to person is

[9]David Hume, *Treatise on Human Understanding* (London, 1888). Quoted in Bryson, op. cit., p. 156.
[10]Bryson, op. cit., p. 160.

built into Adam Ferguson's discussions of instinct and habit. The idea of behaviors being directed by forces preceding knowledge of ends and without any experiential base relating these behaviors as means to these ends—in short, the essential idea of instinct as formulated later by William James and even by many contemporaries—played an important part in Ferguson's thinking. Nevertheless,

> ... the more general character of man's inclinations ... is not that of a blind propensity to the use of means, but instinctive imitation of an end, for the attainment of which he is left to discover and to chuse, by his own observation and experience, the means that may prove effectual.[11]

Thus a person, while having instincts, is in degree freed from those instincts. Humans are generally disposed to innovate. Moreover, apart from inborn instincts, their behavior results from habit, which can scarcely be distinguished from instinctive propensity in that habits are ingrained and seem natural. However ingrained and "natural," they are acquired. And they are acquired largely through human association and through communication from others indicating what is and is not acceptable conduct. If instincts and habit could be separated, though Ferguson says they cannot, he believes it would be shown that habit has a larger role in human behavior than does instinct.

There is a clear connection between the writings of the Scottish moralists and American pragmatic philosophy, from which symbolic interactionism in large measure derives. Much, though certainly not all, of what C. S. Peirce, Josiah Royce, William James, and John Dewey had to say —in particular those segments of their concerns which prefigure ideas and concepts entering symbolic interaction theory—echoes or is anticipated by Ferguson's and Hume's discussions of habit, Hume's and Smith's discussions of sympathy, and so on. More generally, the emphases of these Scottish philosophers on the close relationship of ideas and conduct, the relevance of the natural (including the social) world for the emergence of the individual, the organized and internally dynamic character of the human mind, the susceptibility of the human psyche to study within the framework of science (that is, the treatment of mind and

---

[11]Adam Ferguson, *Principles of Moral and Political Science* (Edinburgh, 1792), Vol. I, pp. 120–128. Quoted in Bryson, op. cit., pp. 139–140.

mental activities as natural objects), and the mind as an instrument for adaption or adjustment, found their way into symbolic interactionism in good part through the work of the pragmatic philosophers, especially the work of James and Dewey.

William James

As Don Martindale notes, James' philosophy was ". . . a device that would permit him to accept mind as an independent reality . . . for reconciling idealism with science."[12] Substantively, the science of James' day was heavily influenced by Darwin and evolutionary theory. In psychology and the social sciences, Darwinism appeared in a variety of ways, one of which was in terms of the concept and the doctrine of "instincts."

In the hands of many, the instinct doctrine emphasized the biologically based, unlearned, and (through experience) unmodifiable character of the behavior of animals, including the human animal. And, as this suggests, the doctrine emphasized the basic continuity between humans and the rest of the animal world. As we later note, this emphasis led many interactionists—in the interests of declaring the independence of man and society from biological determinants—to argue a qualitative gap between man and the remainder of the animal world by declaring that only man had true capacities to manipulate symbols.

For the moment, however, it is the emphasis on unlearned and unmodifiable behavior that is of interest. While James did not reject, and indeed made considerable use of instinct doctrines, his treatment of the role and significance of habit in human behavior constituted an important attack on and modification of then-current instinct theories.

James' discussions of habit begin with a consideration of instincts as the faculty to produce certain ends, without foresight of these ends and without prior learning.[13] Rather

[12]Don Martindale, *The Nature and Types of Sociological Theory* (Boston: Houghton Mifflin, 1960), p. 301. This section makes use of my earlier attempt to deal with the historical development of symbolic interactionist theory: see Stryker, "The Interactional and Situational Approaches," op. cit.

[13]William James, *Principles of Psychology*, (New York: Holt, 1890), Vol.II, p. 383. There is a good, succinct discussion of James' treatment of habit and its relation to the doctrine of instincts in Bernard N. Meltzer, John W. Petras, and Larry T. Reynolds, *Symbolic Interactionism: Genesis, Varieties and Criticism* (London: Routledge & Kegan Paul, 1975). I make use of that discussion here.

than building a motivational theory out of this conception, James uses it as a starting point in arguing the need to see how instincts are superseded by habit: behavior learned and modified (and modifiable) by experience. The basis of habit is memory, through which the human can call to mind the performance of a prior act that has led to some end. Repetition of that act, on the basis of memory, means that the act is no longer blind with respect to its ends; and in time, the instincts disappear. Thus, instincts are both modifiable and transitive: many are destined to "fade away."[14]

The concept of habit as James treats it plays an important role in turning discussion away from biology and toward society in seeking the determinants of and constraints on human actions. Even more important, perhaps, by way of preparing for new insights into the relation of man and society, is James' discussion of "consciousness" and the further discussion of the types of "self" that grew out of consciousness.

The self, according to James, is "the sum total of all that an individual can call his."[15] Involved in this conception is the recognition that human beings can and do develop attitudes toward and feelings about themselves and can see themselves as they see any other object in the external world. Just as humans can denote symbolically other persons and parts of the world around them, can develop feelings and construct responses toward those objects, so too can they respond to themselves. There are four distinct types of self which James elaborates: the material self, the spiritual self, the social self, and pure ego. Obviously, for present purposes, it is the social self that requires further consideration.

Three particularities in James' discussion of the social self are worth emphasis here. The first is the recognition that at least some aspects of the self have an empirical source, and further that the source—in the case of the social

---

[14]Ibid., pp. 390-398. There is a close parallel between the argument James develops with respect to the relation of habit and instincts, and the argument made later by Gordon Allport with respect to the functional autonomy of motives. Gordon W. Allport, *Personality: A Psychological Interpretation* (New York: Holt, 1937).

[15]Ibid., p. 291.

self—is specifically in the recognition given one by others. That view of self, along with another that becomes of special importance in the most recent developments of symbolic interaction theory, is clearly stated in the following:

> Properly speaking, a man has as *many social selves as there are individuals who recognize him* and carry an image of him in their mind. To wound any one of these images of his, is to wound him. But as the individuals who carry the images fall naturally into classes, we may practically say that he has as many different social selves as there are distinct *groups* of persons about whose opinions he cares.[16]

Thus, along with conceptualizing the social self as a derivative of relationships with others, James prepares the way for a view of self which emphasizes its multifaceted character, a view largely neglected between the time of his writing and the relatively recent present. And he prepares the way for viewing that multifaceted self as the product of a heterogeneously organized society.

The third aspect of James' discussion of the social self to be noted here is only partially contained in the just quoted passage. For James, humans instinctively seek to be recognized by other human beings; they measure their self-worth in these terms. That measure, however, does not simply reflect the recognition of others as it may objectively and rationally exist. Rather, one's self-worth or self-esteem is a function of the ratio of success to pretension. There is both an objective and a subjective basis for self-esteem. The objective basis lies in the recognition one gets from others; the subjective basis is in one's own aspirations. To use a modification of James' example, a man may achieve renown as a foremost speaker of the Greek language, but unless he wants to be such, his self-esteem will not be enhanced.

James Mark Baldwin

George Herbert Mead is by all odds the most significant influence on contemporary symbolic interactionism, and of considerable importance as well are John Dewey and Charles Horton Cooley, in part because of their influence on

[16]Ibid., p. 294.

Mead. A lesser known figure, James Mark Baldwin, assumes importance in the historical stream being described because of his influence on both Dewey and Cooley. Baldwin began with James' view of the self, but modified it by arguing that the entire self was social in its origins. He saw personality as a development of this undifferentiated social self, itself a product of self-other relationships. Specifically, he viewed the relationship between the social and the personal, between society and mind, as moving through a three stage process of self-development in the child. The initial, projective stage involves becoming aware of others, drawing distinctions between them and objects, and differentiating among others—distinguishing between mother and sibling, for example. The second, subjective stage witnesses the emergence of self-consciousness through imitating the behavior of others and learning that there are feeling states associated with such behavior. In the third, ejective stage, the child associates these feeling states with its conceptions of persons and so becomes aware that other persons have feeling states just as it does.[17] As Meltzer, Petras, and Reynolds note, this ejective stage "... provides a foundation on which Cooley's method of sympathetic introspection and Mead's theory of role taking rest."[18]

John Dewey

Many of the contributions of the Scottish moral philosophers we have been tracing through James and Baldwin were adopted and expanded by Dewey. The importance of habit is emphasized in the context of insisting upon an intimate relationship between personality and society. Dewey regarded personality organization as primarily a function of habit; and he regarded social organization as primarily a function of custom. But, as anticipated in Ferguson and in Hume, he took custom to *be* collective habit. The implications are clear: the individual cannot be set in contrast to society; there can be no deep chasm or fundamental opposition between self and social order; and personality necessarily develops within a social context. Nevertheless, suggests Dewey, in an influential caution:

[17]James M. Baldwin, *Mental Development in the Child and the Race* (New York: Macmillan, 1906), p. 17.
[18]Meltzer, Petras, and Reynolds, op. cit., p. 12.

To talk about the priority of "society" to the individual is to indulge in nonsensical metaphysics. But to say that some pre-existing association of human beings is prior to every particular human being who is born into the world is to mention a commonplace.[19]

Habits, then, reflect (to any given person) a prior social order; and they ultimately are the basis of thought and reflection.

Only when a man can already perform an act of standing straight does he know what it is like to have a right posture and only then can he summon the idea required for proper execution. The act must come before the thought, and a habit before the ability to evoke the thought at will.[20]

Dewey's pragmatism is apparent. A defining characteristic of pragmatic philosophy is its stress on the process of human adjustment to environmental conditions. What is unique about human beings is their capacity for thinking. Mind is the process of thinking, and thinking arises in the process of humans adjusting to their environment. Mind (thinking) is instrumental; it is the process of defining objects in one's world, outlining possible modes of conduct, imagining consequences of alternative modes, sorting out and eliminating such conduct as is unlikely to achieve adjustment, and selecting the mode that will lead to it.

... deliberation is a dramatic rehearsal (in imagination) of various competing lines of action.... It is an experiment in making various combinations of selected elements ... to see what the resultant action would be like if it were entered upon.[21]

Dewey used this view of mind as instrumental to argue the import of interaction in the explanation of human behavior; and his argument has considerable contemporary relevance vis-à-vis current behavioristic doctrine in psychology. His paper, "The Reflex Arc Concept in Psychology,"[22] written in 1896, raised the question of what constituted a stimulus. His argument is that a stimulus does not exist outside of the activity being pursued by the person,

[19]John Dewey, *Human Nature and Conduct* (New York: Modern Library, 1930), p. 59.
[20]Ibid., p. 32.
[21]Ibid., p. 190.
[22]John Dewey, "The Reflex Arc in Psychology," *Psychological Review* (July, 1896):357–370.

and that it is *defined* in the context of action rather than being prior to and a cause of that action. Thus, a needle in a haystack is not a stimulus to behavior except in the context of someone's search for that needle. The world that impinges on our senses is a world that ultimately depends on the character of the activity in which we are engaged, and changes when that activity is altered.

There are two other aspects of Dewey's argument to be considered here. Briefly, the first is his rejection of the conception of society as a monolithic structure. Instead, he asserted, society consists of many associations and not a single organization. Associations are the coming together in joint action of persons seeking goods that are enhanced by virtue of being shared. There are, then, as many associations as there are goods to be mutually communicated and participated in; and these are limitless in number.[23]

The second is Dewey's insistence that social science, as well as philosophy, takes everyday situations and problems as its subject matter; and that the validation of social science lies in its applicability to those problems, its ability to offer solutions. Once again, themes present in the writings of the Scottish moral philosophers appear as the immediate forerunners of symbolic interactionism.

Charles Horton Cooley

These same themes, as well as others partially or largely foreshadowed in the thinkers covered to this point, appear in the work of Charles Horton Cooley. Thus far, the thinkers dealt with have been philosophers and psychologists, and it is largely through Cooley that their ideas enter sociology.[24]

The special concern of the sociologist is, according to Cooley, the mental and the subjective, for it is these which are distinctively social. One could deny the centrality of the mental and subjective in human social behavior only by

[23]John Dewey, *Reconstruction in Philosophy* (New York: Holt, 1920), p. 205.

[24]It is apparent to me that Cooley must have known the work of Hume, Ferguson, and especially Adam Smith; note, for example, the strong parallels in his concept of the looking-glass self and what Smith had to say in the passage quoted on p. 18. Yet nowhere in his *Human Nature and Social Order* (New York: Scribner's, 1902), the most appropriate place for such, does he cite any of these men. I do not know what to make of this omission. Cooley does cite James, Baldwin, and Dewey; these are among the few nonliterary sources in his citations.

"dodging life itself."[25] The real person exists in the personal idea. Society is a relationship among personal ideas.

> So far as the study of immediate social relations is concerned the personal idea is the real person. That is to say, it is in this alone that one man exists for another, and acts directly upon his mind. My association with you evidently consists in the relation between my idea of you and the rest of my mind. If there is something in you that is wholly beyond this and makes no impression on me it has no social reality in this relation.... Society, then, in its immediate aspect, *is a relation among personal ideas.* ... Society exists in my mind as the contact and the reciprocal influence of certain ideas named "I," Thomas, Henry, Susan, Bridget, and so on. It exists in your mind as a similar group.[26]

"The imaginations which people have of one another are the solid facts of society."[27] This wholly subjectivist assertion is not surprising, given the view that an association between people consists in the relation of ideas within the mind of one of these persons. It is this way of thinking about social relationships that has been criticized as solipsistic. That is, if imaginations are the solid facts of society, it seems to follow that there are as many societies as there are individual imaginations. If our imaginations differ, how can we get beyond these differences and to what do we refer these differences in order to build general knowledge of society? We will see this question raised again as we deal with contemporary variations in symbolic interaction theory.

Given this way of thinking, it follows that the task of sociology is to observe and interpret mental activities. Since imaginations are ultimately accessible only to those who experience them, it also follows that systematic autobiography becomes the prime "method" of the field. Cooley, however, was not happy with the kind of Cartesian introspection that deliberately isolated the introspector from all social influences. He called, instead, for "sympathetic introspection," a process by which one uses sympathy

[25]Charles H. Cooley, "The Roots of Social Knowledge," *American Journal of Sociology,* 32 (July, 1926):59-79.
[26]Charles H. Cooley, *Human Nature and Social Order,* p. 84.
[27]Ibid., p. 87.

to put oneself into intimate contact with as many different sorts of people as possible, allowing these others to awaken in one's mind imaginations of a life similar to their own, which imaginations one then seeks to recall and to describe. It is in this way, according to Cooley, that one "... is more or less able to understand—always by introspection—children, idiots, criminals, rich and poor, conservative and radical—any phase of human nature not wholly alien to his own."[28]

One must introspect, then, to obtain the solid facts of society, since one finds these in the imagination. These imaginations, says Cooley, are as observable as anything else. Again, however, sociologists must use sympathetic introspection. Insofar as others are not available for intimate contact, the detailed case study or some approximation thereof may be a reasonable substitute. Cooley was among the first to observe very young children—his own—in an attempt to formulate and to verify his ideas about the growth of the self.

Heavily influenced by Darwin, by Spencer (though not in all respects), and by Schäffle, Cooley held an organic view of social life as being a vast tissue of reciprocal activity, made of innumerable differentiated systems, all interwoven and unified so that what takes place in one affects all the rest.[29] In keeping with this organic conception, Cooley saw the individual and society—both consisting of personal ideas—as two sides of the same coin of human life. No society exists independently of individuals, and no individual exists apart from society. The individual and society are simply the distributive and collective aspects of the same thing.

It follows that "... there is no view of the self, that will bear examination, which makes it altogether distinct in our minds from other persons."[30] The self is a social product; it is defined and developed in social interaction. Specifically, it is the product of a process summed up in the phrase

[28]Charles H. Cooley, *Social Organization* (New York: Scribner's, 1909), p. 7. Much later, Cooley was to suggest that the motion picture camera was the method *sine qua non* of sociology, since it could capture totally the social process.

[29]Charles H. Cooley, *Social Process* (New York: Scribner's, 1918), p. 28.

[30]Charles H. Cooley, *Human Nature and Social Order, op. cit.,* pp. 91–92.

"looking glass self." The social reference for the self, says Cooley,

> . . . takes the form of a somewhat definite imagination of how one's self—that is, any idea he appropriates—appears in a particular mind, and the kind of self-feeling one has is determined by the attitude toward this attributed to the other mind. A social self of this sort might be called the reflected or looking glass self.[31]

And our social self has three principal components: our imagining how we appear to another person; our imagining that other person's judgment of our appearance; and some self-feeling, such as pride or mortification, that arises from these imaginations. "We always imagine, and in imagining, share, the judgments of the other mind."[32]

This conceptualization of the self and the way it is formed has a number of important consequences, all of which we have seen in somewhat different guises earlier in this chapter: there is and can be no individuality outside of the social order; individual personality is a "natural" development from existing social life and the state of communication among the persons sharing that life; and, the expectations of others are central to this development.

While, as previously remarked, Cooley saw all of social life as intimately connected, the cradle of self-development is the primary group. Primary groups are the "springs of life" for both the individual and the larger units of social organization; linking the two, it is through them that the self evolves. Characterized by intimacy, face-to-face association, and cooperation, these groups are primary in that ". . . they are fundamental in forming the social nature and ideals of the individual," in that ". . . they give the individual his earliest and completest experience of social unity, . . ." and in that they are the source of more elaborate and complex relationships. The family, the play group, and the neighborhood group are the most important primary

---

[31]Ibid., pp. 151–152. This initial reference to the concept of looking-glass self is followed by a couplet: "Each to each a looking-glass/Reflects the other that doth pass." The couplet has been attributed to Emerson, which seems likely since Cooley draws repeatedly on that foremost apostle of self-reliant individualism, but I have not been able to locate it in Emerson's works.

[32]Ibid., pp. 152–153.

groups, because these are the groups that ". . . are ascendant in the open and plastic time of childhood."[33]

William Isaac Thomas

Don Martindale has observed that "At every critical point Thomas' affinities are with the pragmatists and symbolic interactionists."[34] And as others[35] have noted, a principal difference between Cooley's and Thomas' works was that the former was interested primarily in tracing the emergence of self in childhood, while the latter—as a consequence of his interest in social change and social disorganization—was primarily concerned with the processes through which the adult self came to be redefined.

Many aspects of Thomas' work are at least tangentially relevant to this attempt to trace the development of symbolic interaction theory; for example, his interests in social disorganization and his emphatic denial of the abnormality of such disorganization. But for present purposes, it is specifically his emphasis on the substantive and methodological emphasis on *situations* and on the correlative *definitions of the situation* that is of greatest import. When we add Thomas' view asserting the strategic significance of life histories or personal documents for the developing science of sociology to this emphasis, we have focused on the elements in his work most closely related to the major themes of symbolic interactionism.

It is basic to Thomas' position that any account of human behavior is faulty and incomplete if it fails to cope with the subjective, as well as objective, facts of experience.[36] It is the task of sociology to analyze behavior, the forms taken by the processes of adjustment of people and groups to other

[33]Charles H. Cooley, *Social Organization,* op. cit., pp. 23–27. The concept of primary group is one of the more powerful analytic ideas developed in sociology, but it is often misused. Its misuse frequently takes the form of assuming the primary character of *any* family, peer group or neighborhood group, without noting that such collections of particular persons are primary only insofar as interpersonal relations within them are in fact intimate, etc.

[34]Martindale, op. cit., p. 349.

[35]Meltzer, Petras, and Reynolds, op. cit., p. 22.

[36]To anticipate a later point, many symbolic interactionists, in their stress on the subjective, use Thomas' work inappropriately by failing to recognize that he did not believe it warranted to focus on definitions without also focusing on the objective situation.

people and groups. Adjustment processes necessarily occur in situations; that is, adjustment processes are responses to objective circumstances in which individuals and groups are embedded. But, coming between objective conditions—the situation—and adjustive responses are subjective components of experience: definitions of the situation. Thomas provides a most straightforward, succinct and powerful statement of the significance of the subjective in human life: " ... if men define situations as real, they are real in their consequences."[37]

Thomas believed that the situation itself and definitions of the situation had to enter any account of human behavior:

> The total situation will always contain more and less subjective factors, and the behavior reaction can be studied only in connection with the whole context, i.e., the situation as it exists in verifiable, objective terms, and as it has seemed to exist in terms of the interested persons.[38]

And:

> An adjustive effort of any kind is preceded by a decision to act or not act along a given line, and the decision is itself preceded by a *definition of the situation*, that is to say, an *interpretation*, or *point of view*, and eventually a policy and a behavior pattern.[39]

As Thomas stresses repeatedly, introducing subjective definitions of the situation is required in any explanation precisely because the "same" objective situation does not lead to identical behavior.

Thomas makes abundantly clear the fundamental significance of definitions of the situation in that they precede all "self-determined" acts, and all such acts are dependent on them. The personality of the individual and the individual's "life-policy" issue from them. Children, for example, are always born into an ongoing group that has developed definitions of the general kinds of situations faced and has formulated rules of conduct premised on these definitions: moral codes are the outcome of "successive definitions of

[37]Thomas and Thomas, *The Child in America*, op. cit., pp. 565-567.
[38]Ibid., p. 572.
[39]William I. Thomas, *Primitive Behavior* (New York: McGraw-Hill, 1937), p. 8.

the situation." Children cannot create their own definitions independently of society, or behave in those terms without societal interference. And individual spontaneous definitions and societal definitions will always conflict to some extent because the former tend to be selected in hedonistic terms, i.e., for what they will provide by way of pleasure to the person, while the latter tend to be selected on utilitarian terms, i.e., for their usefulness in achieving some social end. In this frame, the problem of socialization becomes a matter of bringing the person to internalize societal definitions, largely as these are provided through the family. Finally, social as well as personal disorganization are resultants of there being rival social definitions of the situations, none of them fully constraining the person.

Volkart[40] has suggested that at no point in Thomas' career was the key concept of the situation defined with sufficient precision to make it a really useful descriptive or analytic tool. Indeed, the meaning of this key term shifted frequently through the course of Thomas' career. In his classic work with Znaniecki, the situation is conceptualized in terms of attitudes and values.

> The situation is the set of values and attitudes with which the individual or the group has to deal in a process of activity and with regard to which this activity is planned and its results appreciated. Every concrete activity is the solution of a situation. This situation involves three kinds of data: (1) the objective conditions under which the individual or society has to act, that is, the totality of values—economic, social, religious, intellectual, etc.—which at the given moment affect directly or indirectly the conscious status of the individual or the group, (2) the pre-existing attitudes of the individual or the group which at the given moment have an actual influence upon his behavior, and (3) the definition of the situation, that is, the more or less clear conception of the conditions and consciousness of the attitudes.[41]

Later, the term was used to refer to "the situation of social relationships," including "all the institutions and mores,"

[40]Edmund H. Volkart, ed., *Social Behavior and Personality: Contributions of W. I. Thomas to Theory and Research* (New York: Social Science Research Council, 1951), p. 29

[41]William I. Thomas and Florian Znaniecki, *The Polish Peasant in Europe and America* (Boston: Houghton Mifflin, 1918–1920), 5 volumes, Vol. I, p. 68.

as well as values and attitudes.[42] More indicative, albeit less precise, of what Thomas likely had in mind by using the term, is his reference to situations as "the configuration of factors conditioning the behavior reaction."[43]

In methodological terms, Thomas advocated the comparative study of situations as the best approximation of the controlled experiment available to the sociologist. One studied concrete situations encountered by the individual, changes brought about in those situations, and in response to those changes, the adaptive strategies and processes of adjustment used in them. Since situations of necessity include definitions of the situation, some appropriate technique to capture this part of reality must be found. Thomas looked to what he generically called personal documents for this technique. Such documents, in the form of case studies, diaries, life histories, letters, and autobiographies, served to reveal the situation from the point of view of the participants in them. That is, they provided the participants' definitions of the situation in ways that purely observational or statistical studies failed to do; the latter were deficient in that they failed to capture such "meaning."

Nevertheless, Thomas recognized the deficiencies and insufficiencies of personal documents, and the value of more objective procedures. Personal documents could help to indicate the important variables affecting behavior, to suggest hypotheses showing how these variables worked to affect that behavior, and to aid in interpreting mass data. In themselves, however, personal documents could not test and verify hypotheses. For this last purpose, Thomas—the major proponent of the personal document as sociological method—turned to statistical research.[44]

George Herbert Mead

Of all the precursors of symbolic interactionism, none is more important or influential than George Herbert Mead. Indeed, in very considerable degree, Mead's conceptualiza-

---

[42]William I. Thomas, "The Relation of Research to the Social Process," in W. F. G. Swann et al., *Essays on Research in the Social Sciences* (Washington, D. C.: Brookings, 1931), p. 176.

[43]William I. Thomas, "The Behavior Pattern and the Situation," *Publications of the American Sociological Society*, 22 (1927): 1.

[44]Thomas and Thomas, op. cit., pp. 565–567. See also W. I. Thomas, "The Relation of Research to the Social Process," op. cit., p. 190.

tion remains central to all contemporary versions of the framework, and so will enter the next chapters. In order to avoid redundancy, the present treatment will be briefer than Mead's significance, in fact, warrants.

Mead was a philosopher and a psychologist. His influence, however, has been most felt within sociology, having taught a course in social psychology at the University of Chicago when sociology was struggling to define its proper domain and orientation. In good part, as Meltzer, Petras, and Reynolds observe,[45] his influence developed from the nature of the course he taught: he provided a counter to dominant theories of human behavior which gave causal priority to the individual. And, in part, his influence reflects the fact that more than anyone before him, he gives systematic treatment to the key ideas of symbolic interactionism that we have been tracing.

Mead's treatment of these ideas drew on a wide range of intellectual resources.[46] Among these, and in addition to the persons whose work has been discussed in the previous pages, were the German Romantic philosophers Fichte, Schelling, and Hegel,[47] from whom he drew the idea that the person, as a self, determines what the world is for that person; Wilhelm Wundt, whose conception of gesture Mead took as a starting point for elaborating on the mechanisms through which mind, self, and society[48] emerge from social interaction; and John Watson, the prophet of early psychological behaviorism, from whom Mead accepted the challenge of accounting for social psychological phenomena in behavioristic terms. More generally, Mead drew on pragmatism and Darwinism as well as behaviorism. As Turner notes, he took from behaviorism the principle of reinforcement, but he rejected behaviorism's denial of the possibility

[45]Op. Cit., p. 28.

[46]See Bernard Meltzer, *The Social Psychology of George Herbert Mead* (Kalamazoo, Michigan: Center for Sociological Research, Western Michigan University, 1966), pp. 8–9, for an interesting specification of these resources. See also Don Martindale, op. cit., pp. 353–354.

[47]See Mead's discussion of the German Romantics in his *Movements of Thought in the Nineteenth Century*, Merritt H. Moore, ed. (Chicago: University of Chicago Press, 1936).

[48]This is the title given to a compilation of Mead's lecture notes published posthumously, which has served as something of a bible for many symbolic interactionists. See George Herbert Mead, *Mind, Self, and Society*, Charles W. Morris, ed. (Chicago: University of Chicago Press, 1934).

of investigating scientifically the internal dynamics of the mind; he took from pragmatism the notion that organisms are practical creatures who adapt to conditions of their worlds; and he took from Darwinism the argument that behaviors facilitating survival are retained, applying that argument not only to Man as a species but to individual human beings.[49]

However, while Mead gave the elements a somewhat distinctive cast—finding it necessary to criticize severely those whose positions seemed closest to his own[50] —his synthesis made central use of the themes appearing in the work previously described. The close relationship (indeed, the conjoint emergence) of person and society, the importance accorded communication, the focus on the development of self and the significance of self in social interaction—these and other themes in the writings of the Scottish moral philosophers, and especially in James, Dewey, and Cooley are the stuff out of which Mead created his synthesis.

Clearly, basic to Mead's thinking are evolutionary principles.[51] Given the biological fraility of the human being, cooperation is essential for survival; and those actions promoting cooperation, hence survival, are retained, those actions failing to do so, discarded. Mind and the human propensity for symbolic communication are emergents from the evolutionary process, developing in accord with evolutionary principles. True for the species as a whole, this is taken as no less true for the individual human being.

Thus, the basic dictum of Mead's social psychology is: start with the ongoing social process. Mead insists that the study of human behavior is best approached from the standpoint of society defined as an ongoing social process. He wished to study human beings from a scientific stand-

[49]Jonathan Turner, *The Structure of Sociological Theory,* rev. ed., (Homewood, Ill: Dorsey, 1978), pp. 315–316. For a more elaborate treatment of the importance of evolutionary concepts in Mead's thinking, stressing the concept of "emergence," see Anselm Strauss, ed., *The Social Psychology of George Herbert Mead,* (Chicago: University of Chicago Press, 1956), pp. iv–xvi.

[50]George Herbert Mead, "Cooley's Contribution to American Social Thought," American Journal of Sociology, 35 (March, 1930): 693–706, and *Mind, Self, and Society,* op. cit., p. 224. See also Martindale, op. cit., p. 354.

[51]Mead's fundamental view of science as method was formulated as an analogue to the evolutionary process; he saw scientific method as evolutionary process made self-conscious. And he saw human behavior, in ideal form, modeled on the scientific method.

point, but insisted that science could not ignore the fact that human beings have minds. Accepting the demands of a behavioristic psychology, yet unwilling to give up this recognition of mind, he sought to resolve the apparent dilemma through applying his basic dictum: "Social psychology is behavioristic in the sense of starting off with an observable activity—the ongoing dynamic social process, and the social acts which are its component elements—to be studied and analyzed scientifically."[52] Both mind and society are seen as a derivative of that process.

Following Mead's elaboration of this fundamental idea will clarify both his use of themes which appear in prior work and his relevance for current symbolic interactionism. Picking up from Dewey, he argues that persons initiate activity that relate themselves and the environment; that is, the persons do not simply respond to external "stimuli" existing apart from the activity. Activity begins with an impulse without ordained end, and the human seeks to satisfy that impulse by adjusting behavior to the objects in the environment. Those objects become stimuli through functioning in the context of the act, during which they may become defined as relevant to the completion of the act. As one grows increasingly hungry and searches for food, objects in the environment—e.g., leaves or berries or grubs— previously unattended become redefined as food. Stimuli *acquire* meaning in the course of activity.

What holds for the individual acting in relation to the nonhuman environment also holds for social acts, those requiring other humans for completion. Social acts involve two or more persons taking one another into account in the process of satisfying their impulses. It is from these social acts that both personality and organized social behavior develop. The mechanism permitting such developments from the social process is communication through language.

Since social acts occur over a period of time, early parts of an act can come to be taken as indications of parts of the act yet to occur. Such early stages of social acts are termed "gestures"; thus, making a fist is a gesture insofar as it indi-

<hr>

[52]Mead, *Mind, Self, and Society,* op. cit., p. 7.

cates that a punch is to be thrown.[53] Communication between persons involves a "conversation of gestures," i.e., the
use by participants of early stages of one another's acts as
indicators or predictors of later stages. Some gestures, labelled significant symbols, come to mean the same thing to
the person producing them as to the person(s) receiving
them; they "mean the same thing" insofar as they indicate
the same future phases of activity to sender and receiver(s).
It is important to recognize that symbols are, for Mead, be-
haviorially defined. "The meaning of what we are saying is
the tendency to respond to it. You ask somebody to bring a
visitor a chair. You arouse the tendency to get the chair in
the other, but if he is slow to act, you get the chair your-
self."[54]

Thus, symbols develop in the context of social acts, and
they function in the course of completing those acts. Symbols enable people to predict their own and others' behavior
and to anticipate the future course of interaction. They also
enable, through this anticipation, the alteration or adjustment of activities *before* the anticipated behavior has occurred. And insofar as they permit persons to gauge the
consequences of their own actions for others, and others'
actions for themselves, symbols provide for relatively high
degrees of efficiency in cooperative activity.

The "self" develops through the same social process. It is
through this concept that Mead dealt with problems of personality. The self is an emergent from social interaction. As
"that which can be an object to itself," the self is essentially
a social structure, and it arises in social experience. In these
terms, the self may be said to exist in the activity of viewing
oneself reflexively. This activity is made possible by language, a system of significant symbols; language permits
use of the standpoint of others in order to view oneself as an
object.

Taking the standpoint of others, "role-taking," is the process through which the self is built. Role-taking, or taking
the role of the other, has been previously described as antic-

[53]Not all acts are carried to completion; they may be inhibited. Thus not all
gestures are consummated through later stages of acts; but this is another part of
the story.
[54]Mead, *Mind, Self, and Society,* op. cit., p. 67.

ipating others' responses on the basis of common participation in a communication process. Anticipated responses with respect to oneself become the part of the self Mead calls the "me." This part of the self is the equivalent of social roles which are the organized attitudes or expectations of others incorporated into the self. It is this part of the self through which one's behavior takes on consistency, since one's actions are mediated through the self.[55]

The other part of the self Mead calls the "I." The "I" together with the "me" make up personality as it emerges from the social process. The "I" represents the responses of the person to the organized attitudes of others, and Mead uses this concept to deal with the creativity and spontaneity he believed to be an important segment of the human experience. For Mead, neither creativity nor spontaneity occur outside the social process; the social control exercized through the "me" part of the self is a necessary condition for their occurrence. Similarly, control by others and self-control are not contradictory, but equivalent emergents from the social process.

Mead viewed the self as developing in two general stages. The initial, "play" stage, begins the process of learning the attitudes of others. In play—being someone else, whether parent, imaginary friend, favorite relative, or television character—the child takes the role of particular others. Organized social life, however, is complex and requires one to learn to take one's place in a complicated social process. To aid in understanding how this is accomplished, Mead offered the metaphor of the "game." In a game, a player must respond to an intricate pattern of related behaviors by others if he or she is to participate effectively. He or she must take the role of the generalized other in order to become part of a complex social process. Again, it is the symbolic capabilities of human beings which permit taking the role of the particular or generalized other. It is pertinent to add that Mead, qua philosopher, held a vision of mankind as an ultimate member of a single "universe of discourse" in which all participated cooperatively in moving mankind to higher evolutionary levels.

On a more mundane level, the individual human being is,

---

[55]Jonathan Turner, op. cit., p. 318.

for Mead, a reflective, self-conscious and self-controlling person. These characteristics are made possible by participation in interaction and through the language communication presupposed by that interaction. One thinks through the manipulation of language symbols. Self-consciousness occurs through viewing oneself from the perspectives or standpoints of others. One controls his or her own behavior by choosing an action from alternatives symbolically present in one's experience.

That selves arise out of the interaction of persons in groups implies the prior existence of such groups. But, according to Mead, the self continuously reacts (through an "I-me" dialectic) to the society that shapes the self. Through this process, society is continuously being created and re-created; it is never fixed. Social order and social change are both aspects of a larger social process.

We have traced the major intellectual stream culminating with contemporary symbolic interactionism. And, for at least one variant of that tradition,—identified with Herbert Blumer—what has been done would be sufficient. But there is another variant for which the historical roots thus far described do not suffice and for which no single figure is so preeminent that he or she would serve to identify it.[56] To oversimplify, it is a variant of symbolic interactionism that merges into a somewhat different historical tradition—that of role theory. Thus, sufficient of the role theoretic traditon must be traced to motivate and justify the description of contemporary symbolic interaction theory presented in the next chapter. The "merger" occurred as some symbolic interactionists became aware that while Mead's schema was reasonably adequate to deal with the emergence of the social person, it was not adequate to treat the complexities of "society" and of the person-society pairing. It is one thing, according to this version of symbolic interactionism, to recognize the constructed character and emergent quality of social life and to retain a view of the individual that recognizes some creative potential in human existence; it is another to deny the reality of social structure as an already emerged patterning of social life that acts as a constraint on the ways in which actors construct their lines of interac-

---

[56]Ralph Turner may be approaching this status.

tion. To put the matter another way, the dictum—accepted by all symbolic interactionists—that both person and society are abstractions from interaction, are (in Cooley's terms) two sides of the same coin, need not be taken to imply that "society" cannot be analyzed in its own terms. Or, to make the point in still another way, the argument that actors' definitions of the situation must be taken into account in understanding behavior does not justify treating society as though it had no substance apart from those definitions. Perhaps an illustration will help: there is an objective reality and import to the distribution of wealth and power (part of the structure of a society) which, while entering personal actions in part through actors' definitions, will affect actions, whatever personal definitions may exist.

For some symbolic interactionists, then (and the author is one of them), the intellectual tasks of a sociology require going beyond what Mead and the tradition reviewed thus far have offered, and require seeking to develop conceptualizations of society consistent with the tradition of Mead but more adequate to sociological concerns. And, to meet these needs, role theory has been utilized. We will try to prepare the way for specifying what it is in role theory that symbolic interactionists have adapted to their sociological concerns by introducing the work of Georg Simmel, Max Weber, and Ralph Linton.[57]

George Simmel

For Simmel, the task of sociology is defined in these terms:

> Sociology asks what happens to men and by what rules they behave, not insofar as they unfold their understandable indi-

[57]In introducing these theorists into the discussion, I do not mean to imply that each has been directly important to the development of symbolic interactionism historically. Indeed, Ralph Turner (personal communication) has suggested that Weber's preoccupation with the distinction between rational and nonrational action has been generally unpalatable to symbolic interactionists and helps account for their failure to use his work more than they do. Weber is introduced here along with Simmel and Linton because they have strongly influenced role theory and are therefore relevant to the attempt to merge traditional symbolic interactionism and role theory; and because by doing so I can emphasize the linkages between the special concerns of symbolic interaction theory and more general sociological concerns. That Weber and Mead do not make such strange bedfellows is indicated by that neglected classic, Hans Gerth and C. Wright Mills, *Character and Social Structure* (New York: Harcourt, Brace, 1953). This next section draws heavily on my prior work, "Fundamental Principles of Social Interaction," in Neil Smelser, ed., *Sociology* (New York: Wiley, 1973).

vidual existences in their totalities, but insofar as they form groups and are determined by their group existence because of their interaction.[58]

As this passage indicates, Simmel did not see all of human behavior as the product of group memberships or of social relationships, a view which leaves ample room for a variety of other kinds of constraints and determinants. However, he did see much of human behavior in these terms, and sociology is that discipline whose objective it is to investigage human behavior insofar as it is shaped by interaction. Simmel clearly has a view of society thoroughly compatible with that of interactionism: society is neither a mere collection of individuals (and in that sense a fiction), nor an entity existing apart from individuals. It is, rather, "the name for a number of individuals, connected by interaction."[59] The study of society thus becomes the study of human association, or the forms of sociation.

Among the social forms to be investigated by sociology are social processes, social types, and developmental patterns.[60] Social processes are stable forms of interaction, and stable forms of interaction define a social structure. "In principle, the forms of sociation are specific roles, statuses, and norms, viewed as reciprocities and as they occur in historical complexes. Conversely, the theory of social structure is merely a theory of form per se."[61]

By "sociation" Simmel means the interaction of minds, the conscious association of persons. Asking how such sociation is possible, his answer emphasizes an interactionist view of person and society which anticipates the ideas of symbolic interaction theory and role theory. Sociation requires the individual be in some degree "generalized": the individual must be both more than and less than an

[58]Georg Simmel, *The Sociology of Georg Simmel,* Kurt H. Wolff, trans. and ed., (Glencoe, Ill.: The Free Press, 1950), p. 11.

[59]Ibid., p. 10. Simmel is identified as a "formal" sociologist. His interests were in the analysis of social forms, which can be thought of as the geometry of social relationships, rather than in the analysis of the content of interaction per se. That is, for example, he wished to know what could be said about (say) conflict as a form of sociation, whether this conflict occurred in the context of a family, between nations, or among community organizations, and as a form independent of just what the conflict is about—love, land, or power.

[60]See Donald H. Levine, "Some Key Problems in Simmel's work," in Lewis A. Coser, ed., *Georg Simmel,* (Englewood Cliffs, N.J.: Prentice-Hall, 1965), pp. 98–104.

[61]F. H. Tenbruk, "Formal Sociology," in Lewis A. Coser, ed., *Georg Simmel,* (Englewood Cliffs, N.J.: Prentice-Hall, 1965), p. 81.

individual personality to be a part of society. The person enters society by exchanging some part of his or her individuality for the generality demanded by the parts he or she is to play. Nevertheless, the individual is unique by virtue of all the social relationships entered and by virtue of orientations to social relationships. Stable social relationships are possible because society appears to the person as a set of "vocations," positions that are in principle capable of being filled by anyone. In this sense the positions are "generalized." But persons are motivated to move into such positions and accept the requirements of society through an "inner call." Persons and social forms—the structure of society—are involved in a dialectic relationship: each shapes and modifies the other. Forms develop in interaction, and that implies that there is always an element of spontaneity, creativity, or novelty in human action which serves to alter social structure. The person is, for Simmel, a social being though not an automaton.

> As individuals we form the personality out of particular elements of life, each of which has arisen from, or is interwoven with society. . . . There is here a reciprocal relation between the subjective and the objective. As the person becomes affiliated with a social group, he surrenders himself to it. A synthesis of such subjective affiliations creates a group in an objective sense. But the person also regains his individuality because his pattern of participation is unique; hence the fact of multiple group-participation creates in turn a new subjective element. Causal determination of, and purposive action by, the individual appear as two sides of the same coin.[62]

Max Weber

The intellectual tradition of German philosophy and social science to which Simmel was in part responding, was also the context against which Max Weber developed his view of sociology. That intellectual tradition starkly contrasted the world of "nature" to which the methodological canons of natural science applied, along with the objective categories of cause and effect, and the world of "human behavior" to which the canons of natural science did not apply and

---

[62]Georg Simmel, *Conflict and the Web of Group Affiliations,* Kurt H. Wolff and Reinhard Bendix, trans., (Glencoe, Ill.: The Free Press, 1955), pp. 140–141.

which required understanding in terms of the subjective
motivations underlying behavior. According to this tradition, subjective motivations could only be grasped through
precise historical detail. Weber combined in his work rejection of a purely historical approach and acceptance of the
demand that sociology view human action from the point of
view of the human actors it studied. He insisted that general theoretical concepts were essential to the knowledge of
human behavior, and this implies that one must ignore at
least some elements of concrete, historical events to which
these concepts refer if we are to achieve knowledge. Thus,
Weber insisted on a sociology that is true to its subject matter without giving up the effort to be scientific.

> Sociology ... is a science which attempts the interpretive
> understanding of social action in order to arrive at a causal
> explanation of its course and effect. In "action" is included
> all human behavior when and in so far as the acting individ-
> ual attaches a subjective meaning to it.[63]

An action is interpretively understood when it is placed
in a motivational context, i.e., when one discovers what
would adequately motivate the behavior of the actor. This
means entering the experience of actors in situations in
order to see things from their perspectives, a methodological directive closely akin to that implied in Thomas' concept of definitions of the situation. One does so through the
method of *Verstehen,* roughly translated as sympathetic
understanding and obviously related to Cooley's method of
sympathetic introspection. We understand when we see the
ends the action seeks to achieve and the actor's means to
those ends. We understand the man aiming a gun if we find
out that he is a member of a firing squad ordered to shoot,
that he is a soldier fighting an enemy, or that he is seeking
revenge. It is important to note Weber's awareness that not
all human behavior is motivated, that many nonmotivated
factors affect human action which both actor and analyst
must take into account, and that there are not only means
and ends of action from the point of view of the actor to be

[63]Max Weber, *Max Weber: The Theory of Social and Economic Organization,*
A. M. Henderson and Talcott Parsons trans., (Glencoe, Ill.: The Free Press, 1947),
p. 88.

taken into account but also conditions: "favouring or hindering circumstances."[64]

While Weber's sociological fame rests largely on his typology of social action, based on the concept of "rationality" as applied to the ends and the means of action, and on the application of this typology in underscoring the bases for legitimacy in social relationships, for present purposes it is his development of the concept of social action and the extension of that concept to the social relationship that is most important.

For Weber, behavior constitutes social action when that behavior has a subjective meaning attached to it. A "social relationship" exists when each of a number of actors take one another into account in orienting or directing their actions. Mutual "taking into account" is the defining characteristic of a social relationship, which exists only as a probability that the subjective meanings involved will lead to a certain type of action. The action can be quite diverse —friendship, attraction, hostility, conflict—and is not necessarily reciprocal in the sense of meanings being shared: one's definition of the other as a lover is not always reciprocated. Social relationships can change in subjective meaning over time; that is, their bases can be altered: a relationship based on commonality of interests can shift to one in which interests conflict.

Weber raises the question: under what circumstances will social relationships maintain the particular forms they take? His answer is in terms of a typology of social action based on the concept of "rationality"; the conscious weighing of alternatives with respect to both the ends and the means of action. Social relationships maintain their form through expediency—the need of actors for one another to achieve their ends. They will more likely endure, however, when they are supported by custom and habit. And they are most likely to do so when they are accorded legitimacy, when the rules underlying the relationships are taken as binding. Such legitimacy can be accorded social relationships through tradition, emotion, belief in an absolute value, or by virtue of some process recognized as legal. The relevance of these aspects of Weber's thought to an emer-

[64]Ibid., pp. 93–95.

gent symbolic interactionist framework will be remarked in the summary of this chapter.

Ralph Linton

There is a long line of anthropological writing which finds exceptionally clear and straightforward expression in the work of Ralph Linton.[65] He begins with a conception of society as "... any group of people who have lived and worked together long enough to get themselves organized and to think of themselves as a social unity with well-defined limits."[66] Societies require for their survival the adaptation and organization of the individuals who compose them. Over time, adaptation takes the form of a well worked out and stabilized division of labor, with increasingly predictable and increasingly complete and effective cooperative behavior among the members of a society. Although individuals are under certain conditions capable of altering society, they are, nevertheless, thoroughly dominated by society which perpetuates through constant training the mutual adaptations in behavior making cooperative life possible.

Given this vision of the way societies work, a key question is what guides the training of the members of society? Linton's answer is "ideal patterns." These ideal patterns are remembered and rationalized experiences of adapting to the environment in which the society exists. They are systems of ideas guiding individuals in situations for which they have not been trained, serving as well as guides to training individuals. They become valued within a society. Further, they are held up as models for behavior and thus help shape behavior into approximations of themselves. While ideal patterns are never completely found in behavior, behavior in all social relationships is influenced by them. They have a supraindividual quality, surviving the persons who exhibit or promote them.

All cultures have ideal patterns guiding the relationships between persons or between classes of persons. The essence of such patterns is reciprocity: persons *A* and *B* engage in

[65]Especially in Ralph Linton, *The Study of Man* (New York: Appleton-Century, 1936).
[66]Ibid., p. 91.

different but complementary behaviors creating a circular flow of rights and duties from which each draws benefits. The same basic reciprocity holds for the individual in relation to society; Linton's example concerns the man giving up a place in a lifeboat for a woman, acting as an agent of society and reciprocating for society the services that women as a class render to it.

As this example suggests, categories of persons can occupy polar positions in reciprocal ideal patterns. Those occupying positions are accorded rights and obligations in relation to others occupying complementary positions. Every person will be involved in many such reciprocities. The totality of ideal patterns guiding the relationships between persons in a society and between society and the individual constitute a social system. This means, for Linton, that a society will seek to make situations of conflict rare; it will not require conflicting duties of the person, or will it allow constant conflict in the ideal patterns which guide assigned activities.

Linton calls the polar positions in the ideal patterns for reciprocal behavior "statuses." A status is a position in a particular pattern, a position occupied by a person who also occupies other statuses at the same time. It is a collection of rights and duties, the dynamic aspect of which (a status in action) is a "role." All persons in a society play numerous roles, as well as a general role which sums the particular roles played and which determines what persons do for society and what they may expect from society.

The concepts of status and role serve to reduce ideal patterns to individual terms. In so doing, they organize individual attitudes and behavior so that these are congruent. In Linton's view, "It is obvious that, as long as there is no interference from external sources, the more perfectly the members of a society are adjusted to their statuses and roles, the more smoothly the society will function."[67] In addition to anticipating minimal conflict, either within individuals or between persons in society, as a consequence of the nature of statuses and roles, Linton anticipates minimal difficulties in filling statuses and obtaining adequate role performances in spite of individual differences among hu-

[67]Ibid., pp. 114–115.

man beings: "Fortunately, human beings are so mutable that almost any normal individual can be trained to the adequate performance of almost any role."[68]

Summary

It is apparent that symbolic interactionism has had a long and diverse "history," in the sense that there have been a large number of persons contributing to its current state. No complete enumeration, much less discussion, of contributors has been attempted.[69] Rather, a major stream of development beginning with the Scottish moral philosophers and culminating with George Herbert Mead has been described, as has a second, merging stream introducing more structural concerns than evident in the first. In connection with the latter, Simmel, Weber, and Linton have been briefly reviewed.

Each of the persons covered has made a substantial though not necessarily unique contribution to symbolic interactionist thinking, a contribution that will be apparent in the following two chapters. The Scottish moral philosophers, collectively, established the legitimacy of treating man as a natural object and the scientific import of everyday experience. They initiated an approach to human behavior from the standpoint of society, argued the import of habit relative to instinct and the relation of habit to custom, and saw mind as an instrument for adaptation. Their stress on communication, and in particular on sympathy, foreshadowed the interactionist's view of the basic nature of society and of the origin of the self.

William James, in his treatment of habit, iterated the need to turn to society as the source of determinants and

---

[68]Ibid., p. 115.

[69]It is not possible to list all who have been left out. A number of contemporary contributors omitted, and the reasons for their omission, were noted in Chapter 1. Two others whose influence on symbolic interactionism broadly conceived has been substantial, in their attempts to handle the difficult concept of motivation as well as in other ways, are the literary critic Kenneth Burke and the sociologist C. Wright Mills. See, in particular, Kenneth Burke, *A Grammar of Motives,* (Englewood Cliffs, N.J.: Prentice-Hall, 1945); C. Wright Mills, "Situated Actions and Vocabularies of Motive," *American Sociological Review,* 5 (December, 1940): 904–913.

constraints on behavior. His conception of the self as multifaceted, of the social self as the product of relations with
others, and of the character and sources of self-esteem, anticipated a series of relatively recent developments in
thinking about the relation of person to society.

Baldwin added depth to views of the process through
which relationships between mind and society and between
the personal and the social develop in childhood, and so
added depth to extant conceptions of personality development.

Apart from reinforcing the lessons to be learned from
James and Baldwin, Dewey's insistence on the priority of
society to person, of the way in which humans shape the
world they respond to by defining stimuli in the context of
their activity, and on society as a set of many, differentiated
associations, add considerably to the stock-in-trade of the
interactionist.

It is Cooley's emphasis on the underlying identity of person and society that is perhaps his major contribution. But
important as well is his stress on communication as the link
among men making society possible, his insistence that the
"self" is critical to human behavior, and his view of primary groups as wellsprings of human development.

More than any other thinker, Mead showed the primacy
of interaction in shaping minds, selves, and societies. He,
above all others, established the symbolic character of human interaction. His treatment of the significance of language processes, his view of the self as a social product, and
his vision of social behavior as including the indeterminate
outcome of the dialectic between the "I" and the "me" are
noteworthy as well.

Simmel gives us a view of society as sociation, as interaction; and he presents society as a structure of positions (vocations) carrying expectations to be met by persons who fill
them. Still, he recognizes the uniqueness of every individual, and in so doing is able to see social life as both stable
and changing, with persons reproducing tradition and expected patterns, and contributing novelty and change into
organized social life.

Highly influential has been Weber's demand that sociology be both a generalizing science and responsive to the

subjective aspects of social life. His insistence that sociological explanation requires grasping the meanings underlying social action and the development of typologies of social
action that point up the possibilities for reflective self-control in human behavior, and his emphasis on legitimacy
which implies the centrality of values and norms in struc-
turing social behavior, have been equally influential.

Linton's conception of "ideal patterns" also emphasizes
the central importance of norms in accounting for organized social life. And his conception of society as a structure
of positions (statuses) and roles tied together through reciprocal ideal patterns, his recognition that persons occupy
many positions and play many roles, and his observation
that the function of socialization is to make society "work"
are all significant in the development of the symbolic interactionist perspective.

Were the interest of this present chapter to trace the heritage of symbolic interactionism completely, the story could
neither begin with the Scottish moral philosophers nor end
with Ralph Linton. Perhaps the most serious omission, is an
extended treatment of Robert E. Park. Park's position in the
story is particularly interesting since he taught at the University of Chicago while Mead was still there, he studied
with William James at Harvard and briefly with Simmel in
Berlin, and he influenced generations of sociologists
through his position at the University of Chicago and
through the classic *Introduction to the Science of Society.*[70]
It is particularly interesting as well because his work seeks
to link the social psychological concerns of Mead with the
broader concerns of sociology by using the concept of role
to discuss the relationships of self and social structure.
Thus his writing is peculiarly appropriate as a bridge to the
next chapter in which a version of symbolic interactionism
is presented which tries to carry that task forward.

> The conceptions which men form of themselves seem to de-
> pend upon their vocations, and in general upon the role they
> seek to play in communities and social groups in which they
> live, as well as upon the recognition and status which society

[70]Robert E. Park and Ernest W. Burgess, *Introduction to the Science of Society*
(Chicago: University of Chicago Press, 1921).

accords them in these roles. It is status, i.e., recognition by the community, that confers upon the individual the character of a person, since a person is an individual who has status, not necessarily legal, but social.[71]

[71]Robert E. Park, *Society* (New York: The Free Press, 1955), pp. 285–286. I have never seen a treatment of symbolic interactionism that sees Park as a central figure in its development. Perhaps his role will be more generally appreciated as interactionists place their concerns with self, emergent definitions of the situation, and interaction in broader structural contexts.

3

Contemporary Symbolic Interactionism: A Statement

Introduction

The title of this chapter is misleading insofar as it implies that there is a single set of ideas that all who call themselves symbolic interactionists would accept without question and to the same degree. Fortunately (from the point of view of the continued development of the theory), such is not the case. There are, rather, varieties of symbolic interactionists—a subset will be discussed in the next chapter —each taking a somewhat different stance with respect to critical theoretical, conceptual, and methodological issues. Given the range of differences that exist, had the attempt been made to restrict this book to a "central" version of contemporary symbolic interactionism upon which all symbolic interactionists agree, this would be a very brief chapter indeed!

Rather than restrict the chapter's statement to matters of universal or even general agreement, our aim is to present the author's version of symbolic interactionism. It largely omits methodological issues of considerable import from consideration. These issues have been referred to in Chapter I and will be reintroduced when reviewing variations on the "central" themes in subsequent chapters. It is, perhaps, with respect to methodological issues—how we are to conduct our inquiries to achieve the goals we as social scien-

51

tists seek to achieve—that differences internal to symbolic interactionism are most sharply drawn.

The author's version of symbolic interactionism is by no means idiosyncratic; but many who are symbolic interactionists will quarrel with aspects of it and some will quarrel with its general thrust. This version begins with Mead, but goes beyond Mead to introduce role theoretic concepts and principles, in order to adequately deal with the reciprocal impact of social person and social structure. The nexus in this reciprocal impact is interaction. It is in the context of the social process—the ongoing patterns of interaction joining individual actors—that social structure operates to constrain the conceptions of self, the definitions of the situation, and the behavioral opportunities and repertoires that bound and guide the interaction that takes place. Or, as Weinstein and Tanur[1] put it, social structure makes available for any encounter the resources for any constructed definition of the situation. And it is in the interaction that takes place that social structure itself is fundamentally changed, modified, elaborated on, or reaffirmed.[2]

The version of symbolic interactionism to be sketched, then, incorporates elements of role theory. The point of articulation is in the concept of "role." One way of representing both the complementarity and the differences between symbolic interactionism (as it developed historically) and role theory (as that framework developed) is to suggest that each uses this brick-building concept. Primarily interested in the twin problems of personal organization and disorganization, in issues of socialization, and in the analysis of

[1]Eugene A. Weinstein and Judith M. Tanur, "Meanings, Purposes and Structural Resources in Social Interaction," *The Cornell Journal of Social Relations,* 11 (Spring, 1976):105–110.

[2]The intent of these statements is to note both the potential for change and the potential for stability in the relation of person and social structure. To emphasize the constructed character of actual interaciton is neither to say that what is contructed is necessarily different from what previously existed, nor that it necessarily simply reproduces what existed. Both stability and change—of person and of society—are part of the social world with which sociology must come to grips; both are "real." The important questions become, under what conditions does social structure so constrain interaction that novelty is at a minimum; under what conditions is the larger social structure resistant or even impervious to alteration through the medium of interaction; or conversely, under what conditions is novelty or creativity in interaction maximized, and under what conditions is social structure maximally open to the impact of altered interactive episodes?

the interaction process itself, symbolic interactionism used a role concept to build "down" to the social person and to the level of personality structure. Oriented principally to problems of social organization and change, in the analysis of interaction relevant to groups, intergroup relations, and larger units of social organization, role theory used the concept to build "up" to larger and more complex social units.

A satisfactory theoretical framework must bridge social structure and person, must be able to move from the level of the person to that of large-scale social structure and back again. A most important lesson to be learned from the intellectual sources of symbolic interactionism is that a focus on the person without a correlative focus on social structure, or vice versa, is necessarily partial and incomplete. A continual theme in Simmel, Cooley, and especially Mead is that social structure creates social persons who (re)create social structure who ... ad infinitum. But that insight, basic as it is to an understanding of social life, becomes trite and trivial unless it leads to research which specifies both variations in social structure and variations in social persons as well as the connectives among these variations. To accomplish such research, there must exist a conceptual framework facilitating movement across the levels of organization and person.

Where one starts in providing such a framework is arbitrary. As a practical matter, everyone is born into an ongoing social system of some sort and so looking first at the impact of society on the person is appropriate. However, the fundamental reciprocity of society and the person ought not be forgotten.

A generalized version of the framework to be explicated in the remainder of the chapter can be stated:[3]

1. Behavior is dependent upon a named or classified world. The names or class terms attached to aspects of the environment, both physical and social, carry meaning in the form of shared behavioral expecta-

[3]Segments of this generalized statement of symbolic interactionism appear in Sheldon Stryker, "Identity Salience and Role Performance: The Relevance of Symbolic Interaction Theory for Family Research," *Journal of Marriage and the Family*, 30 (November, 1968,):558–564.

tions[4] that grow out of social interaction. From interaction with others, one learns how to classify objects one comes in contact with and in that process also learns how one is expected to behave with reference to those objects.

2. Among the class terms learned in interaction are the symbols that are used to designate "positions," which are the relatively stable, morphological components of social structure.[5] These positions carry the shared behavioral expectations that are conventionally labeled "roles."

3. Persons who act in the context of organized patterns of behavior, i.e., in the context of social structure, name one another in the sense of recognizing one another as occupants of positions. When they name one another they invoke expectations with regard to each other's behavior.

4. Persons acting in the context of organized behavior apply names to themselves as well. These reflexively applied positional designations, which become part of the "self," create internalized expectations with regard to their own behavior.

5. When entering interactive situations, persons define the situation by applying names to it, to the other participants in the interaction, to themselves, and to particular features within the situation, and use the resulting definition to organize their own behavior accordingly.

6. Social behavior is not, however, determined by these

[4]How symbols come to carry shared meaning can, of course, be a topic for research in its own right. That is, the development of shared meaning may be taken as problematic and is taken as such by those who work the ethnomethodological vein. By and large, however, symbolic interactionists take the existence of significant symbols—names or class terms carrying shared meaning—for granted, recognizing however that the fact of shared meaning or the degree to which meaning is shared are always open questions. The justification for assuming the existence of meanings shared, in important (sufficient) degree, lies in the commonsense observation that many relatively stable, social relationships exist but could not if there were not some minimum of shared meanings. These observations, it may be noted, make the point that symbolic interactionism and ethnomethodology are not in opposition; they ask different questions and therefore take different starting points.

[5]Role theory deriving from Linton has used the term "status" rather than "position" for this purpose. Given the hierarchical implications of "status" and the intent to refer to nonhierarchical as well as hierarchical components of social structure, the term "position" seems preferable.

definitions, though early definitions may constrain the possibilities for alternative definitions to emerge from interaction. Behavior is the product of a role-making process,[6] initiated by expectations invoked in the process of defining situations, but developing through a tentative, sometimes extremely subtle, probing interchange among actors that can reshape the form and the content of the interaction.

7. The degree to which roles are "made" rather than simply "played," as well as the constituent elements entering the construction of roles, will depend on the larger social structures in which interactive situations are embedded. Some structures are "open," others relatively "closed" with respect to novelty in roles and in role enactments or performances. All structures impose some limits on the kinds of definitions that may be called into play and thus limit the possibilities for interaction.

8. To the degree roles are made rather than only played as given, changes can occur in the character of definitions, in the names and class terms those definitions use, and in the possibilities for interaction; and such changes can in turn lead to changes in the larger social structures within which interactions take place.

One version of contemporary symbolic interaction theory is largely, if not totally, contained in this brief set of statements. The statements can be given greater depth through a consideration of major concepts which are either explicitly or implicitly contained in them and through a consideration of underlying principles.[7]

The Social Person

We may start with the observation that humans live in physical, biological, and social worlds that provide the ends to which human activity is oriented as well as the means by

[6]The term is Ralph Turner's. See his "Role-taking: Process versus Conformity," in Arnold M. Rose, ed., *Human Nature and Social Processes,* (Boston: Houghton Mifflin, 1962), pp. 20–40.

[7]For an earlier statement in part reformulated here, see Sheldon Stryker, "Fundamental Principles of Social Interaction," in Neil Smelser, ed., *Sociology,* Second Edition (New York: Wiley, 1973), pp. 495–547.

which those ends are (or are not) achieved. These worlds represent conditions that are or can be taken into account by actors seeking their ends, conditions that can guarantee, enhance, impede, or deny the success of their efforts. They offer actors opportunities for activity and they make more or less probable contact with others with whom cooperation or conflict may result as they act with reference to their ends. They supply the resources used in interaction and sometimes create problem-posing situations which require novel behavioral solutions.

Language and other symbolic systems incorporate terms that refer to various aspects of these worlds in ways that represent meanings for human action. These terms are often, though not necessarily, generalizations of behavior toward objects: they are class terms or categories. Humans respond not to the naive world, but to the world as categorized or classified; the physical, biological, and social environment in which they live is a symbolic environment.[8] The symbols that attach to the environment have meaning, are cues to behavior, and organize behavior.

Much human behavior is habitual, that is to say, not problematic. Such behavior does not call for active effort to symbolically represent the environment, although such symbolic representations may be the product of prior generations of humans—i.e., be completely a matter of custom— or the product of earlier (and "successful") behaviors of a person. When, however, one enters a situation in which behavior is problematic—when pure custom or pure habit does not suffice—one must find some way to symbolically represent the situation if one's behavior is not to be essentially random or completely arbitrary. One must, in short, come to some definition of the situation.

Symbols focus attention upon salient elements in an interactive situation, and permit preliminary organization of behavior appropriate to it. Culture may be thought of, from this perspective, as a specification of what is important for interaction by being relevant to goal-oriented activity, a specification representing the cumulative experience of a social unit. As this observation implies, there are frequently

---

[8]There is no claim here that if part of this environment is not symbolized, it has no effect on human behavior. The only claim being made is that unless that part has meaning and is at least preliminarily symbolized, human actions cannot be organized with reference to it.

ready-made definitions available as quickly as appropriate cues are perceived.

Frequently, however, and particularly in periods of rapid social change, prior generations will not have experienced many situations so there exists no ready-made definitions in fully articulated form. Even where cultural definitions exist, actors either may not have experienced some situations or been made aware of the extant cultural definitons. Therefore, there will be the need to construct definitions either before or upon entering situations. Whether preexistent or constructed anew, definitions typically undergo some revision in the process of interaction itself as initial definitions are tested against the realities of the situation and reformulated in each experience. Interactions with others serve to validate or challenge definitions. They are vehicles of conflict among competing definitions, and are structured by such further definitions as emerge from the interactions themselves. Indeed, it is not unreasonable to conceptualize such interaction as involving a "battle"—sometimes relatively benign and sometimes not—over whose and which definitions are to prevail as the basis for future interaction.

Defining a situation involves naming aspects of the non-human environment; it also involves a process of naming others and naming oneself. A discussion of the former leads directly to the concept of role.

ROLE

Role theory proper has used the concept of "status" or "position" to refer to the parts of organized social groups. Symbolic interactionism uses "position" in a more general sense, to refer to any socially recognized category of actors. In this usage, positions are symbols for the kinds of persons it is possible to be in society: rich man, poor man, thief, fool, teacher, sergeant, intellectual, rebel, president, and so on and on. Like other symbolic categories, positions serve to cue behavior and so act as predictors of the behavior of persons who are placed into a category. Doing so, they organize behavior with reference to these persons. Attaching a positional label to a person leads to expected behaviors from that person and to behavior toward that person premised on expectations. The term "role" is used for these expectations which are attached to positions.

This usage has a number of implications. Roles are social

in the same sense any other symbolic behavior is social: Shared behavior defines the positions to which roles attach themselves. They are social as well in the specific sense that one cannot use the language of roles without at least implicit reference to counterroles: there can be no employer without employee, no mother without child, no professor without student.

Clearly, the expectations which constitute roles can vary in many ways potentially important to interaction processes. They can carry little or no normative freight or be heavily ladened with insistent norms. When they are normatively defined, sanctions for failure to meet their requirements can range from trivial to strong. Expectations can be general or specific; they can require precise performance of specific behaviors or can simply exist in the form of an outline within which a great deal of improvisation can take place; they can be very clear in their demands or vague and uncertain; they can apply to a minimal segment of one's range of interactions or across the whole of that range; they may attach to positions in formally organized social structures or relate to informal social relationships. Much of the theoretical work yet to be accomplished by symbolic interactionists will relate such variations to the processes and outcomes of social interaction.

Since societies are complex and differentiated systems, persons are typically categorized in terms of multiple positions at least some of which are likely to provide conflicting or contradictory cues to behavior and consequently acquire no clear expectations or means of organizing responses. Elaboration on some of the consequences of this relationship between social structure and person will follow.

Actors entering situations categorize others in ways relevant to defining the situation and behaving in it. So, too, actors will typically—though not necessarily[9]—categorize themselves and respond to themselves by naming, classify-

---

[9]This caution is meant to imply that self-reflective behavior is variable in its occurrence in interaction. In the philosophic point of view from which symbolic interactionism derives, thinking occurs as a response to a problematic situation. The self-reflective activity labelled "self" is a form of thinking. The implication is clear: where situations are totally unproblematic (perhaps a *very* rare event in modern society), there may be no self. Here is one point on which the present treatment of symbolic interactionism departs from conventional treatments and is (perhaps) unique.

ing, and defining who and what they are. To engage in such reflexive behavior is to have a self.

SELF

Mead's definition of the self as that which is an object to itself is simply an elliptical way of suggesting that one can and sometimes does view oneself objectively, that is from the standpoint of others with whom one interacts, and that this reflexive activity has consequences for behavior. The reality of the self is phenomenological, and is based on reflexive activity; it has no physical or biological location.

Self-definitional activity proceeds largely, though not exclusively, through socially recognized categories and corresponding roles. Since roles necessarily imply relationships to others, so does the self. "One's self is the way one describes to himself his relationships to other in a social process."[10]   Along with James, Mead recognized that the human being has many selves, as many as there are separate organized groups responding to the person, but apart from the distinction between the "I" and the "me," went no further in elaborating a self-structure. Indeed, his focus as well as that of most who follow him is on self as an undifferentiated unity, a focus consistent with his hope for an ultimate universal community of mankind. Short of that universal community, the principle that *self reflects society* requires a view of self that corresponds with the realities of the contemporary complexities of society.[11] That is, if social relationships are complex, there must be a parallel complexity in the self.

Apart from this requirement based on theoretical principle, there are empirical issues whose resolution calls for a conception of self as complex and differentiated, albeit organized, rather than an undifferentiated unity.[12] Some give higher priority to work than to recreation in exercising

[10]Sheldon Stryker, "Interactional and Situational Approaches," op. cit., p. 138.

[11]See the discussion in Meltzer, Petras, and Reynolds, op. cit., pp. 94–95, for a comparison and opposing evaluation of these two quite different ways of conceptualizing the self. An empirical study seems to show that there are correlates of these differing views of self, i.e., that different views of the nature of social organization, social control, etc., tend to go along with each. See Larry T. Reynolds and C. McCart, "The Institutional Basis of Theoretical Diversity," *Sociological Focus*, 5 (Spring, 1972):16–39.

[12]See Sheldon Stryker, "Identity Salience and Role Performance," op. cit., for the initial elaboration of these ideas.

choice with respect to activities; others reverse the priority. A man uses his free time to play golf rather than opting to take his child to the zoo. Under circumstances in which having both marriage and a career is not feasible, one woman chooses to pursue a career rather than to marry, another makes the opposite choice. The analysis of the behaviors represented in these illustrative observations is advanced by a conception of self which is elaborated in ways that go beyond but remain in the spirit of Mead's conceptualization.

This elaboration introduces a new set of concepts: identity (or role identity), [13] identity salience, and commitment. Identities are "parts" of self, internalized positional designations. They exist insofar as the person is a participant in structured role relationships. In Gregory Stone's terms, one has an identity when one is placed as a social object by others in the same terms that one appropriates and announces for oneself.[14] One may have a long list of identities, limited only by the number of structured role relationships one is involved in. Thus, a woman may have identities as physician, wife, mother, child, tennis player, Democrat, etc., which taken together comprise the self.[15]

"Identity salience" is intended to refer to one possible, theoretically important way in which the self can be organized.[16] Discrete identities may be thought of as ordered

[13]This is a term used by Burke and also by McCall and Simmons. Equivalent to the concept of identity as used here, the intimate linkage of self and role is emphasized by the term. See Peter J. Burke and Judy Tully, "The Measurement of Role/Identity," *Social Forces,* 55 (June, 1977): 881–897 and George J. McCall and J.L. Simmons, *Identities and Interaction,* Second Edition, (New York: The Free Press, 1978).

[14]Gregory Stone, "Appearance and the Self," in *Human Behavior and Social Processes,* op. cit., pp. 93–94.

[15]Obviously, the self defined in these terms incorporates a great deal of raw material. This is a much delimited conception of self, however, compared with those which make the self equivalent to the sum of all possible self-referencing assertions. Too, this conception of self slights one possible way to conceive of Mead's "I," as pure impulse. It retains a principle of novelty and creativity in the self by playing off various identities against one another. Creativity is seen as being made possible by the existence of multiple identities, including some which may exist as "memories of former 'me's" and which may exist only through symbolic reference to future role relationships.

[16]A second way, which will not be pursued here, is in terms of alternative modalities of self-reflexive behavior. Identities are cognitive responses to oneself as an object. Alternatively, one can respond to oneself in conative "I want" and cathectic "I feel" terms. Presumably there are systematic (or organized) relationships among these modalities of self-response. It may be that a most reasonable approach to the "I" aspect of self can be made through these alternative ways of responding to self.

into a salience hierarchy, such that the higher the identity in that hierarchy, the more likely that the identity will be invoked in a given situation or in many situations; this probability of invocation is what defines identity salience.

Not all situations invoke more than one identity, but it is likely that an identity's location in a salience hierarchy will lower or raise its "call-up" threshold in interaction with other defining characteristics of situations; indeed, this is directly implied by the definition of identity salience. To the degree that a situation is structurally isolated—has no implications for other interactive situations—it is less likely that more than one identity will be invoked. But to the degree that there is structural overlap among situations—i.e., when analytically distinct sets of social relationships do impact with one another—different identities are likely to be concurrently called up. If different identities are called up, they may or may not carry conflicting or contradictory expectations. If they do, their relative location in the identity salience hierarchy becomes a potentially important predictor of subsequent behavior.

The notions that situations may be structurally isolated or that they may structurally overlap with other situations, and that these social structural characteristics affect the makeup of the self, reintroduce the underlying symbolic interactionist premise that self reflects society. Now, however, the pursuit of the intimate connectives between society and self is allowed to move to new levels of precision. Greater precision in specifying linkages between society and social person is also made possible through the concept of "commitment." Not analytically part of the concept of self, commitment is one way of conceptualizing aspects of social structure closely related to self structure which can permit the development of predictive theoretical propositions from the conceptual framework of symbolic interactionism.

To the degree that one's relationships to specified sets of other persons depend on being a particular kind of person, one is committed to being that kind of person.[17] If the maintenance of ties to a set of others is important to the person,

---

[17]This way of conceptualizing commitment is based on Kornhauser's use of the term in analyzing the retention and loss of membership in political groups. See William Kornhauser, "Social Bases of Political Commitment: A Study of Liberals and Radicals," in Arnold M. Rose, ed., op. cit., pp. 321–329.

and dependent upon being—say—a member of a sorority, that person is committed to being a member of a sorority. Since entering into social relationships is premised on the attribution and acceptance of positions and associated roles, then commitments are premised on identities.

ROLE-TAKING AND SOCIALIZATION

The expectations of others serve to define roles and are important to the structure of the self. Situations must be defined, and this entails recognizing physical and behavioral cues in the settings of interaction as well as locating self and others within the settings. How do we come to know, even very provisionally, the expectations of others? And how do we learn the meaning of features in the environment, the kind of person it is possible to be in a given society or in given subunits of that society; the roles that attach to positions, those one may occupy oneself and counterpositions as well; the permissible variations built into roles, and so on? The symbolic interactionist's response to such questions uses the concepts of role-taking and of socialization.

One takes the role of others by using symbols to put oneself in another's place and to view the world as others do.[18] Role-taking is the process of anticipating the responses of others with whom one is involved in social interaction. Making use of symbolic cues present in the situation of interaction, prior experience, and familiarity with the particular other or with comparable others, one organizes a definition of others' attitudes, orientations and future responses which is then validated, invalidated, or reshaped in ongoing interaction. Actors take the role of others to anticipate the consequences of possible patterns of action they can initiate and they take the role of others to monitor the results of their actions. Using the results of their role-taking, they sustain, modify, or redirect their own behavior.

[18]Clearly, the role-taking concept relates closely to the notion of sympathy as used by the Scottish moral philosophers. Insofar as "sympathy" or related concepts (empathy) emphasize a sharing of the feeling tones of others, they diverge from the intended meaning of role-taking, which focuses on the prediciton of others' future behavior. Implied here is the argument that role-taking is fundamental to all interaction, whether cooperative or conflictive, whether one intends to use the information gained through the process to help or destroy the other. To effectively engage in war, one must anticipate the responses of the enemy in the same manner as a parent must anticipate the responses of a child when seeking to aid the child through a crisis.

Accuracy in role-taking is based at least in part on common experience which creates a fund of common symbols; but accuracy in role-taking is variable. The fact that organized social life exists at all is presumptive evidence of shared meanings; there is no assumption being made, however, that meaning is either universally or completely shared. Nor is there any assumption which necessarily relates accuracy in role-taking to the smoothness and cooperativeness of interpersonal relations. On the one hand, ignorance of the other can permit interaction to continue when accurate role-taking may threaten a relationship; where there is differential vulnerability or differential dependency in a relationship, for example, information may be screened out lest it disrupt the relationship.[19] On the other hand, conflict may well sharpen the accuracy of interpersonal perceptions by increasing sensitivity to nuances in the role-taking process.

Role-taking is one way persons learn how others locate them and of others' expectations for their behavior. But there is a larger process through which this and related learning takes place: socialization. Socialization is the generic term used to refer to the processes by which the newcomer—the infant, the rookie, the trainee, the freshman—becomes incorporated into organized patterns of interaction.

In a sense, every interaction provides a socializing experience. One is in part socialized by responding to the expectations of others. Others, deliberately or not, cast one into a role and provide the symbolic cues that serve to elicit expected behavior. Such altercasting[20] is a form of coaching, a sometimes formal, sometimes informal process through which much socialization occurs. Many roles are learned through playing the roles, frequently though not always prior to actually occupying a position. Given the capacity for symbolic behavior, it is possible to engage in anticipatory socialization—to imaginatively be another, to learn vicariously how to act in various situations, to try out roles. Much education takes the form of anticipatory socializa-

[19]Sheldon Stryker, "Role-taking Accuracy and Adjustment," *Sociometry*, 20 (December, 1957):286–296.

[20]The term is Eugene Weinstein's. See Eugene A. Weinstein and Paul Deutschberger, "Some Dimensions of Altercasting," *Sociometry*, 26 (December, 1963): 454–466.

tion. One learns as well through imitation, perhaps gradually accruing meanings while "going through the motions," while copying the behavior of one or another role model.

If every interaction serves to socialize, then socialization is a continuous, lifelong process. Early socialization of the infant and the child is of particular significance, however, for once a self has been formed through the interactive process it serves to modify subsequent experience. Later socialization is likely to involve destroying early identities in order that newer identities can be formed. The principles already discussed suggest that this can be effectively done to the degree that commitments to interactional networks supporting the early identities can be cut.[21]

Sociologists have sometimes used the term socialization to refer only to processes that induce persons to conform to the ideals of a society; in this usage, one is socialized only insofar as one is brought to share the values and norms of what Linton called the ideal patterns of a society.[22] There is no question that socialization does have this social control function. To the degree that the person comes to incorporate societal definitions of appropriate role behavior into self and to internalize as salient identities given social positions and their accompanying expectations, the person is effectively controlled. There are at least two mechanisms implicated in this process. In the first place, it is reasonable to assume that persons will generally seek confirmation or validation of their identities—at least their highly salient identities—by behaving in ways that elicit validating responses from others. Thus, having an identity which is premised on societal definitions will tend to produce behavior that conforms to those definitions. In the second place, it is also reasonable to assume that in general, people want to think well of themselves. In brief, self-esteem becomes tied to behaving in accord with a salient identity. When that identity is defined in terms that reflect the norms and values of society generally, or some segment of society, conforming behavior is also esteem-producing behavior.

[21]The classic study of the phenomena, although not discussed in these terms, is in Sanford Dornbusch, "The Military Academy as an Assimilating Institution," *Social Forces,* 33 (May, 1955):316–321.

[22]It is this notion of socialization and the theoretical framework underlying it that Dennis Wrong criticizes so effectively in his "The Oversocialized Conception of Man in Modern Sociology," *American Sociological Review,* 26 (April, 1961): 184–193.

But the processes of learning to conform are not fundamentally different from the processes through which one learns to be independent or to nonconform, to deviate from ideal patterns. A highly differentiated society, in which conflict is endemic and in which interactional systems premised on different norms and values coexist within the same larger societal framework, makes it possible for socialization to result in conformity but in nonconformity and deviance as well.

Under discussion has been the social person, and the focus has been on the ways in which the individual comes to have a self and to define situations. Necessary to the discussion of the social person, however, has been a discussion of position and role. And the point is iterated once again: there can be no sociological reference to the social person without coordinate reference to at least some aspects of social organization. The concepts of position and role are at the same time basic to a discussion of the person and to a discussion of social structure.

Social Structure

To invoke the idea of social structure is to refer to the patterned regularities that characterize most human interaction. Whatever may be true of the creative potential of persons in their interactions with one another, as a matter of empirical fact most of their interactions tend to be with the same or only slowly changing casts of others,[23] and the same sets of persons tend to be bound together or linked[24] in interactional networks doing essentially the same things

[23]This way of stating the matter slights the distinction between interactions that occur among the same concrete persons (e.g., members of some particular family) and those that occur between differing persons who nevertheless may be conceptualized as the "same" social objects (e.g., clerks in a department store and a continuously changing set of customers). For many purposes, this distinction has considerable import, but not for the present discussion.

[24]The terms "bound" and "linked" are intended to refer to two quite different patterns, both of which are covered by the notion of social structure. The former term refers, in the extreme case, to a set of persons all of whom interact with one another in some defined situation or situations; some families would serve as an illustration. The latter term, again in the extreme case, refers to a chain of relationships in which each person serves to link two and only two others neither of whom interacts with the other. A variant of the latter is what Merton called a "role-set." See Robert K. Merton, "The Role-Set: Problems in Sociological Theory," *British Journal of Sociology,* 8 (May, 1957):106–120. A role-set is that complement of persons who are linked by virtue of their common tie to the occupant of some social position, e.g., students, parents, administrators, and school board members, who have a common tie to a teacher in the school system.

on a repetitive basis. Thus, the concepts of group, organization, community, etc., indicate aspects of social life in which subsets of persons are tied together in patterned interactions and are separated (at least with respect to those interactions) from other persons.

As part of the "patterned regularities" to which it refers, social structure also references the more abstract social boundaries that crosscut all societies, but particularly large, industrialized, contemporary societies. So, for example, any society is likely to have a class structure, a power structure, an age structure, an ethnic structure, and so on.

In any case, the important implication of the generic concept of social structure is that societies are differentiated entities, and that as a consequence of that differentiation it is only certain people who interact with one another in certain ways and in certain settings or situations. That is, the concrete interactions that are the ultimate referent of all sociological and social psychological constructs do not relate persons randomly, nor are the opportunities for and the circumstances of the relationships that take place randomly distributed.

Thus, if the social person is shaped by interaction, it is social structure that shapes the possibilities for interaction and so, ultimately, the person. Conversely, if the social person creatively alters patterns of interaction, those altered patterns can ultimately change social structure. The defining task of a sociologically oriented social psychologist is precisely to specify the principle contained in the former assertion. One of the important tasks[25] of sociology per se is to develop the latter assertion. And, overall, the promise of a sociology will not be met until the bridging of social person and social structure required by both of these objectives can be readily accomplished. It is to that end symbolic interactionism adapts and incorporates aspects of role theory.

[25]Also among these tasks, some would say the defining task of the sociologist, is to specify the sources and consequences of relationships among groups and institutional structures within a society and between societies. While such specification can take place without reference to the social persons whose behavior is abstracted when a concept like group, institution, or society is used, surely a better understanding will have been accomplished when the person can in fact be incorporated.

SYSTEM

The referent of the term "system" is to anything that can be analyzed into a set of parts so that one part is in some way dependent on each of the remaining parts. Any science—and sociology is no exception—concerns itself with establishing and accounting for relationships among those "parts" it takes as its special purview. Thus, any science must take as a working assumption that such relationships exist. There is no need to assume that the dependency of one part on others is total, nor that the "package" of parts upon which a particular science focuses includes all of those affecting in some (possibly important) way the parts that are in the package. And the working assumption that there are systemic relationships in what a science studies must ultimately be justified empirically through the demonstration of interdependency.

The system concept has implicitly been utilized in the earlier discussion. To suggest that the self can be conceptualized as a set of discrete identities organized into a hierarchy of salience is to say that the self is a system composed of interrelated parts. To regard social interaction as involving the complex interplay of preexistent selves, definitions of others, definitions of the situation, and so on, is again to assume that social interaction is a system composed of interrelated parts. Now, in pursuing relevant aspects of role theory, it can be said that society can be regarded as a system and the question becomes: how can its parts be specified?

The starting point is again with social interaction. Interactions among persons vary in their duration, frequency, periodicity, and significance both for the persons involved and for others with whom these persons may connect. Some interactions are short in duration and tenuous: two persons who say "hello" to one another as they meet in passing on the street. Others last longer and have greater significance for the actors involved: the relationships of doctor and patient, employer and employee, parent and child. Interactions of all kinds that repeat themselves, but especially those that last and are important to participants, will develop expectations with respect to the proprieties that are to be observed in the interactions. They tend to be labelled, and the labels carry behavioral meanings part of which are norms specifying the proper mode of relationships between persons in ongoing patterns of interaction. As earlier noted, these norms can vary along a number of dimensions including their specificity.

Interactions also vary in the degree to which they link together persons who are (or are not) in large measure also linked to one another. [26] The concept of "group" can be used to refer to networks of interaction in which there is a high degree of "closure" in the sense that the persons involved all tend to interact with one another, a recognition of common membership in an organized unit and a sense of interdependency with respect to common goals. It is important to recognize that groups, so conceived, are structures of interaction: while all interactions do not have characteristics of groups, all groups are systems of interaction. It is also important to recognize that no limits are being put on the kinds of interactions involved. Groups may be structured by either cooperative or conflictful interactions; typically they include both.

Groups are systems of interpersonal relationships which tend to be normatively defined, or to contain normative elements. Norms—the oughts, shoulds and musts of social life —that operate within a group do not necessarily apply in the same way to all members of the group. Husband is not expected to behave in relation to wife as wife is expected to behave in relation to husband, and the norms affecting spousal relationships are not the norms affecting the relationships of parent and child. Norms defining the reciprocal rights and duties of "status unequals" in the context of a bureaucratic organization are not identical with those defining the rights and duties of "status equals". Groups, then, are structures of *differentiated* relationships: they are structures of positions and roles.[27]

That groups can be and are conceptualized as structures

[26]Obviously, the referent here is to interactions among more than two persons.

[27]Traditional role theory has used these terms with different nuances when compared with their usage by symbolic interactionists. Since role theory is more concerned with describing social structure as it is at any point in time rather than as it develops, with the implications of action systems for society in general, and with strongly institutionalized patterns of interaction, it has used "position" to refer to the differentiated parts of organized groups, formal associations, etc., rather than extending the term to the full range of "the kinds of people it is possible to be" within a society. And role theory attaches more of a firm, fixed quality to the normative aspects of role.

of positions and roles, provides the point of articulation between social structure and social person, for the latter too has been so conceptualized. This commonality connecting person and structure is what gives symbolic interactionism the theoretical means to begin specifying the transactions between the two, to begin making more precise than is otherwise possible propositions concerning the impact of society on individual and vice versa.

Groups, then, are units of social structure; they are not, however, all that is connoted by "social structure." The stock-in-trade of sociology includes notions like community, social class, ethnicity, kinship systems, political institutions, religious institutions, and the like, including society. And if the promise of the preceding paragraph is to be met, these "larger" aspects of social structure must be incorporated into the theoretical framework.

While a full-fledged development of how such incorporation could proceed is beyond the scope of the present work, possibilities can be sketched. Social life is interaction. Most interaction takes place within the boundaries of groups or as performances of persons acting as representatives or agents of groups. The relevance of larger social structures lies in the ways they impact on interaction and on the formation, maintenance, or dissolution of groups; and it lies in the ways interaction and group formation, maintenance or dissolution impact on these larger structures. In general, that relevance is in the form of affecting the probabilities of particular kinds of persons coming into contact in particular kinds of situational settings, and in affecting the probabilities that interaction will take on particular form and content.[28]

Thus, the larger society defines the inventory of the kinds of people it is possible to become; one cannot become a professional athlete in a society which does not provide for athletic competition on a professional basis, and the opportunity to become a soccer player in America today is present in a degree it was not a decade ago. Perhaps more importantly, the evaluational meanings attached to positions that influence the efforts to become one or another kind of per-

[28]Indeed, one way of defining (or of ascertaining the existence of) social structures is precisely in terms of the degree to which such probabilities are affected.

son reflect the rewards available in society for attaining these positions. In the same terms, social class alters the probability of becoming—say—a physician by the way it distributes the means, financial and otherwise, for achieving higher education.

The sociological significance of age, class, ethnicity, ecology, or other structural elements in a society lies in part in their impact on just who is brought into contact with whom, that is to say, the interactions that do in fact occur, and in their impact on the kinds of interaction that occur. In general, schools bring together persons of roughly the same age and the same class background; thus, the probability of friendship relationships that cross age and class boundaries is less than it might otherwise be. One can only marry someone one meets, and one is much more likely to meet someone living in the same section of a community. Interactions occuring between blacks and whites are more likely to be superficial and conflict laden if the educational, residential and occupational structures in a community are essentially segregated. Deviant work schedules or work settings that isolate work crews from the community at large, constrain interactions to take place between those who share the deviant schedule or the work setting.

As the foregoing discussion implies, it has long been observed that groups—voluntary associations, families, sports teams, etc.—tend to be formed of persons sharing some structural characteristic. If, then, norms grow out of and reflect participation in groups, the larger social structure will in important degree specify the norms that persons bring to their interactions, both with others inside the groups to which they belong and with others outside those groups. Again, the character of interactions—cooperative, conflictful, or whatever—will be in part contrained by the larger structure.

More generally, the meanings that persons learn to attach to objects in their world—including themselves—are largely learned through their interactions with others. To the degree, then, that age, class, or other social structures affect group formation and maintenance and resultant interactions, these social structures enter the entire system of meanings of actors.

And, as earlier suggested, structure provides the resources that persons use in their interactions with others. A community organization provides the setting in which the highly educated citizen uses her knowledge of *Roberts' Rules of Order* to keep an opposition spokesman from challenging a ruling. The expensive clothes of an upper-class businessman both symbolize and reinforce claims to dominance in an interaction with a skilled worker. The middle-class child learns politeness and courtesy which can be used to advantage in dealing with secondary others in formal, institutional settings. Institutionalized rules of deference in the relationship of teacher and pupil enable the former to exercise power that might otherwise have little legitimacy.

It should be emphasized that the resources for interactions made available through social structure are important whether roles are played out in interaction as given or whether they are essentially constructed in the process of interaction. Further, the degree to which roles can be made rather than simply played is variable in part as a function of social structure. There is very little room for improvisation in the context of a prison; there is, presumably, a great deal more room for the creative construction of roles in the early stages of a newly formed voluntary association.

Societally imposed scheduling takes the school-aged child out of interaction with family members for long segments of the day throughout much of the year, and introduces the child to possibly competing sets of relationships. Coinciding schedules of band and French classes in a high school force the adolescent to choose one or the other and so creates the opportunity for particular interactions and denies the opportunity for others. The general pattern of scheduling vacations in the summer months creates positions and settings that enable various kinds of interactions to occur; the counselor in the summer camp, the waitress in the beach resort hotel, etc.

Scheduling is one of the social mechanisms available, whether advertently or inadvertently used, to isolate groups (and so provide opportunities for interaction of members) from one another or to guarantee that contact will occur. But other mechanisms exist as well. A definition of a "good husband" and "good father" as one who has a steady and relatively high income insures the overlap of family and work spheres of life. A system of hospitals sponsored and paid for by the Veterans Administration brings medical and veteran groups into certain kinds of relationships. Systems of segregation work to keep various kinds of persons out of touch with one another or to assure that contacts are limited to certain types. Management and worker groups may relate to one another only through the intermediary role of the supervisor, who is both part of and outside of both groups.

This illustrative excursion into the ways in which structural features of a society may be incorporated into a symbolic interactionist framework makes use of conceptual elements not totally prepared for in the discussion preceding it, and anticipates a necessary discussion of the twin concepts of role strain and role conflict. In order to introduce this discussion properly, it is necessary to look back at the concept of group as used within this interactionist frame.

In this usage, groups do not consist of persons as "total" beings; rather, they are composed of parts of persons. True, they may vary considerably in the proportion of the action systems of persons they incorporate: the conventional sociological distinction bctwccn primary groups and secondary groups is based, among other things, on the poles of the implied continuum. But, even groups based strongly on primary relations will not typically absorb all of the person's interpersonal activities.

An obvious and theoretically pregnant characteristic of the relation between person and group emerges at this point: persons are usually members of many groups. From the point of view of the person, the groups to which he or she belongs may have many or few common members; in the extreme, only he or she may connect two otherwise independent groups. From the point of view of the larger social structure, there may be no linkage (no common membership) between any set of groups, minimal linkage, or— in the atypical and extreme case—total overlap in membership. As this discussion suggests, it is possible to visualize sets of groups $(A, B, C, \ldots N)$ each pair of which is connected by a single person $(a, b, c, \ldots n\text{-}1)$ or by varying numbers of persons.

If groups are distinct systems of interaction, and if norms develop in the context of systems of interaction, it is possible that the norms developing in the various groups in which any person participates may be quite different. Whether similar or different, however, the norms affecting interaction within a given group may either support and reinforce or contradict and conflict with the norms affecting interaction within another group; and a person who is a member of both groups may serve to introduce the conflicting sets of norms to both groups, and may reflect in his or her own behavior the conflicting norms.

These observations lead naturally to a consideration of the concepts of role conflict and role strain. These concepts nicely illustrate the interactionist principle that person and society are two sides of the same coin. At the same time, they serve to illustrate the ways in which the symbolic interactionist framework can illuminate the processes through which the person can effect changes in the larger social structure.

ROLE CONFLICT

Role conflict exists when there are contradictory expectations that attach to some position in a social relationship. Such expectations may call for incompatible performances; they may require that one hold two norms or values which logically call for opposing behaviors; or they may demand that one role necessitates the expenditure of time and energy such that it is difficult or even impossible to carry out the obligations of another role. That the person typically occupies many positions and faces many sets of role expectations, and that there are typically many counterroles occupied by many persons which interface with any single position held by that person, create the strong possibility of role conflict. A social structure that consists of partially independent, partially overlapping networks of interaction is fertile soil for the production of role conflict. Insofar as this is true, role conflict needs be seen as a normal product of a complex social structure.

There are varying types and sources of role conflict and it appears that variation in both types and sources relates to how such conflict impacts on the person and to possibilities for resolution.[29] Conflicting expectations may derive from the same other, as when a parent communicates to a child the demand that the child be both a top student and a top athlete. They may come from different others within the same group, or from others who are members of different groups; for the adolescent, the varying expectations of peers and parents illustrates the latter and the different demands of mother and father that may impinge on an offspring illustrates the former. Role conflict may be intra- or interrole. Intrarole conflict, deriving from the contradictory expectations of a single other, may be most difficult for the person to deal with, since there appear to be few mechanisms available for resolving such conflict.

The intensity of role conflict will affect the possibilities for its resolution. The degree of incompatibility between conflicting expectations will make a difference with respect to intensity, as will the rigor with which sanctions are applied to the failure to meet these expectations. Perhaps most relevant to intensity, however, is the degree to which highly salient identities may be involved or the degree to which the conflict implicates the self. One holds expectations for oneself derived from one's identities; one faces the expectations of others as well. If the identity associated with one role is highly salient and the identity associated with a second role lacks salience, then conflicting expectations from others may have very little meaning to the person. If the demands emanating from others are insistent but in conflict with the demands deriving from a highly salient identity, the conflict is likely to be relatively severe.

Withdrawal from the relationships that are the source of conflict is one available mechanism for role conflict resolution.[30] Clearly, constraints of social structure will mean that this mechanism is more or less available in fact; and commitment to networks of others will condition its use. To

[29]For an extended discussion of these issues in the context of an attempt to relate the social psychological literature on role conflict and the social structural literature on status inconsistency, see Sheldon Stryker and Ann Statham Macke, "Status Inconsistency and Role Conflict," *Annual Review of Sociology,* Vol. IV, Ralph H. Turner, James Coleman and Renee C. Fox, eds, (Palo Alto, Calif.: Annual Reviews, Inc., 1978).

[30]See Theodore R. Sarbin and Vernon L. Allen, "Role Theory," *The Handbook of Social Psychology,* Vol. I, Gardner Lindzey and Elliot Aronson, eds., (Reading, Mass.: Addison-Wesley, 1968), p. 542.

some extent, one can choose between the horns of the dilemma, accepting one expectation and rejecting the other. Whether or not this is a viable alternative depends in part on the sources of conflicting expectations; it is feasible when expectations derive from persons in different groups, less feasible when expectations come from the same other or from others within the same group. Again, however, one's freedom to reject the relationships from which the rejected expectations come, as well as one's commitment to those relationships, will affect the likelihood of clear choice. Some creative effort to alter the character of the expectations is also a possibility.

At least some role conflicts are not activiated because it is possible to isolate the conflicting expectations in time or in place. To the degree that work and home can be separated from one another, conflicting expectations from these two sources can be handled relatively effectively. Scheduling and the allocation of different relationships and activities to different time slots can keep conflicting expectations apart. Some creativity may be possible in restructuring either the phasing or the location of one's interactions, should separations of conflicting expectations not be built into the rhythm or spacing of interpersonal relations. As this suggests, once again, social structure will be an important conditioner of possibilities.

The preceding discussion has emphasized the negative potentialities (from the point of view of the individual) in situations of conflicting role expectations; indeed, it has been the pathology of role conflict that has been stressed at least since the early and pioneering writings of Harriet Mowrer.[31] But role conflict has an important creative potential as well. Interactionist writings, from Mead forward, have visualized the possibility of self-control and creativity emerging from adopting the diverse standpoints of multiple others and using these to free oneself from the demands of particular others and/or to arrive at novel solutions to problems.

What is role conflict,from the point of view of the person,

---

[31]Harriet R. Mowrer, *Personality Adjustment and Domestic Discord* (New York: American Book Company, 1935).

is "role strain,"[32] from the point of view of the larger social structure in which the person is located.

ROLE STRAIN

From the point of view of society, there is a continual problem of maintaining the continuity of social roles that underlies the stability of social structure.[33]   Continuity is problematic for a number of reasons: not all persons accept the norms embodied in roles or even presumably central societal values; the degree to which persons are emotionally committed to norms and values is variable; social class and other structural variations in society introduce variations in attachment to norms and values; some persons who accept particular norms and values may also hold contradictory norms and values; emotional attachment to norms can exist without conformity to those norms, and conformity can occur without such attachment; shifts in social positions can mean shifts in behavior and in normative and value orientations; and all persons at some point face conflicts among their values, ideals and role obligations.

Some role strain, defined as a felt difficulty in fulfilling rolc obligations, is omnipresent. Role expectations will not be so pleasurable as to produce automatic conformity. Meeting those expectations will always require the use of energy and of resources, and not always at the time or in the place one wishes to expend energy and resources. Multiple role obligations mean multiple and potentially contradictory obligations. Each role relationship typically calls for several lines of action at least some of which are likely to be inconsistent. And many roles tie the person to a varied set of counterroles which have conflicting interests built

[32]The term is William J. Goode's, and much of the following is drawn from his treatment. See his "A Theory of Role Strain," *American Sociological Review,* 25 (August, 1960):483–496. To some degree, from an interactionist's viewpoint, Goode and others whose focus is primarily on the larger social structure tend to see roles, norms, etc., as clearer and more fixed than they, in general, are; they may even reify these concepts. A symbolic interactionist view serves as a counter-balance to this tendency in its emphasis on the constructed character of roles and norms, just as a structuralist view balances the interactionist's tendency to see everything in continual flux.

[33]This ostensibly "conservative" vision of society need not be such. One could as reasonably assert that from the point of view of society, there is a continual problem of disrupting the continuity of social roles in order to achieve desired social change.

into them: the physician linked to patients, colleagues, hospital administrators, nurses, and interns provides an example.

Given the nature of role relationships, then, the person faces many distracting and sometimes conflicting role expectations so role strain is normal. As Goode puts it: "In general, *the individual's total role obligations are over-demanding.*"[34] The person has the problem of managing an entire system of roles so as to reduce strain to tolerable levels; the larger social structure has the problem of integrating role systems so that institutions can work. The person can use various mechanisms to help reduce strain. Psychological compartmentalization, the delegation of some role obligations to the extent social structures permit delegation, the elimination of some role relationships, restricting interaction by erecting barriers that prevent others from initiating or continuing role relationships, and seeking to establish interactional role bargains that minimize costs—these as well as others treated in the earlier discussion of role conflict—are ways of manipulating role systems to reduce strain.

Social structure operates to increase or decrease individuals' role strain; it also determines, in part, which if any of the mechanisms reviewed can be used and the degree to which they can be used. Definitions of what is and is not adequate as a role performance are supplied by social structure. Structure also provides a hierarchy of evaluations which aids in sorting out role expectations by ordering their priorities; feeding a family, for example, is more important than entertaining it. Third parties who serve to remind one of role obligations are frequently built into social systems; ministers, the police, and other agents of social control often serve this purpose. Role obligations are often structurally linked or structurally dissociated: to be a good father one must meet the obligations of the job; and treating students equitably may be achieved by rules inhibiting the

---

[34]Ibid., p. 484.Emphasis in original. It has been argued that the accumulation of role demands can be beneficial to the person and society rather than a source of psychological stress and social instability, i.e., that role strain is hardly an ubiquitous feature of social life. See Sam D. Sieber, "Toward a theory of role accumulation," *American Sociological Review,* (August, 1974), pp. 567–578. Both positions are likely correct, and the real issue is the conditions (social circumstance, types of role demands, etc.) under which one or the other occurs.

development of teacher-student friendships. Ascribed statuses limit the role-bargaining options of persons.

Since social structures are built out of role relationships, attempts to deal with role strain necessarily affect the structure of society. Depending on how role expectations are or are not met, social systems may be stable or experience great change. Role strains are clearly fateful, not only for the persons who experience them but for the larger social structures containing them as well.

One type of role strain emerges in roles linked to a number of counterroles, a phenomenon Merton defined as a "role-set."[35] The way in which role relationships can affect the larger social structure can be illuminated via this concept. A person occupies a position and is related to other persons playing counterroles through that position. Each counterrole articulates to its own network of relationships: the teacher, for example, links students who in turn are linked to a larger circle of administrators. The teacher can thus serve as a bridge between two larger circles which might otherwise be isolated from each other. If these larger circles hold conflicting definitions, the teacher may experience role conflict or strain. The possibility exists for that conflict or strain to be reduced if the teacher explains one group to the other. If successful, the teacher's personal problem is resolved *and* a social cleavage is mitigated.

Toward a More Adequate Symbolic Interactionist Theory

Recalling the discussion in Chapter 1 of the difference between a theory and a conceptual framework, it is clear that the present chapter has been concerned with the presentation of a symbolic interactionist framework. A general point of view, some assumptions, and a set of concepts which includes suggestions about the various ways behaviors might relate have been offered. What has not been offered is a theory per se; nor can one be offered now. But we can attempt a partial theory, or bits and pieces of a larger theory that will ultimately be forthcoming.

We begin with the generalized symbolic interactionist

[35]Robert K. Merton, op. cit.

model outlined on pp. 53–55. Implied by the assertion that social behavior is not simply given by expectations but is the product of a role-making process, is the further assertion that the enactment or performance of a role is variable, that there may be some choice in whether or not to perform a role and that there may be the opportunity to reject the expectations attached to a position occupied or to modify the performance called for. If that is so, an important empirical question becomes, what is it that influences timing and performance of a role?

The close, mutually determinative relation of self and society that is basic to symbolic interactionism now comes into play. The sociological conception of "society" incorporates the idea of patterned, organized interaction. Asking how, or in what terms, society is patterned has led sociology to an image of society in terms of positions and roles. Given that the person is the other side of the society coin, then this view of society leads to an image of the person as a structure of positions and roles which, internalized, is the self.

If, however, society and self literally reproduce one another, the relationship between society and the individual must be a totally static relationship. Our sense, of course, is that this relationship is anything but static; and the issue now becomes how to deal conceptually, theroretically, and analytically with a dynamic relationship between society and individual. In part, sociology has responded to this issue by building complexities into our image of society: society is conceptualized as multifaceted, composed of disparate levels, groups, and institutions whose relationships run the gamut from cooperation through conflict, and a mosaic of interdependent but highly differentiated parts. Given that we recognize complexities in our image of society, it follows that we must recognize complexities in our image of the person and thus of the self.

In part, too, the sociological response to this issue has been to recognize that not all interactive behavior is captured by the concept of society, and to recognize that the self has a structure that does not simply reproduce the interactive behavior that is captured in the concept of society. That is, only some part of human interaction is describable in terms of a structure of positions and roles; and, since both self and society derive from interaction, only part of the self is describable in these terms.

What has been said thus far is translatable into a simple system, a model of which is:

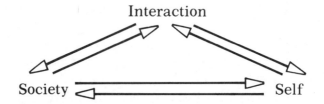

Presumably this system is not instantaneously reciprocal; it makes sense to lay out a temporal sequence, recognizing nevertheless, the existence of feedback loops. This is simply to assert that any of the three major concepts may be the focus of attempts at explanation. Frequently enough, social psychologists have been interested in the self as a dependent variable, most often treating that facet of self termed self-esteem. If interested in explaining interaction, then, our model would assert (given that some segment of time is isolated):

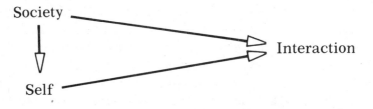

The debt of this model to Mead's argument, that it is reasonable to put society before self, should be obvious; for any given person it is the case, certainly, that existing society antedates the emergence of self.

This simple model restates the central issue for those whose work stems from a symbolic interactionist framework and for those who wish to consider seriously the possibility that the self is cause rather than consequence of behavior. It asserts that the self is necessary to account for interaction. If we revert to the argument that both society and self are complex phenomena, we come to the further assertion that the import of the self in explaining interaction will be variable. In brief, the degree to which this simple model will accord with the evidence, will depend on the particulars of society, self, and interaction that we attempt to link. Just what those particulars of import may be has not been well explored, though there are suggestions in a variety of sources[36] including the previous sections of this chapter.

Ideally, it would be possible at this point to provide an exhaustive catalog of facets, dimensions, and aspects of the three major variables of the model. Given that exhaustive catalog, the work of theory would involve systematic specification of hypotheses linking a particular facet of society with a particular dimension of self with a particular aspect of interaction. Since that exhaustive catalog does not exist, theory building can proceed in a different manner, by limiting attention to particularized translations of the major variables that appear to be theoretically promising or strategic.

Commitment, as previously defined, represents one way of conceiving the relevance for interaction of society as an organized system of positions and roles. An earlier statement[37] noted two dimensions of commitment: the sheer number of relations entered, or extensivity; and the depth of relations entered, or intensivity. Also suggested was a measurement strategy in terms of the "costs" of giving up meaningful relations to others should alternative role choices be made. Commitment, as a particularized translation of "society," focuses on social networks: the number of others to whom one relates through occupancy of a given position; the "importance" of others to whom one relates through occupancy of a given position; and the multiplexity of linkages, that is, the number of distinctive kinds of activities attached to a particular linkage to another or others. The concept of commitment can lead as deeply into social networks as a theorist is prepared to go.

Identity salience is one specification of the concept of self and the earlier discussion of this concept need not be repeated. A second specification is in terms of self-esteem. It seems reasonable to believe that self-esteem will intervene

[36]See, in particular, McCall and Simmons, op. cit.; Stryker, "Identity Salience and Role Performance," op. cit.; Goode, op. cit.
[37]Stryker, "Identity Salience and Role Performance," op. cit.

in the relation of identity structure to behavior. Identity salience and esteem are "formal" aspects of the self, in that they make no reference to the content or meaning of self. It is possible and certainly will be ultimately necessary to refine our positional concepts and consequently our identity concepts by noting that there are multiple ways of being a spouse; for example, the terms partner, companion, and provider are used by some family sociologists in describing possible spousal roles.

If it is recognized that not all interaction reflects positions and accompanying expectations, but that important segments of interaction do, attention can be narrowed to role performances.[38] That obviously still leaves a very complex variable; thus, it is necessary to ask, what are the dimensions or aspects or types of role performance that can be expected, on theoretical grounds, to reflect the separate or joint effects of society and self?

The question with which this section began provides one answer: role choice behavior, including entry into a position (or positions) or selection of a role among roles to play when options are open; seeking out and discovering, or creating, opportunities to enact a role; selection of persons with whom one can interact from among a larger set of possible others who are appropriate others for particular role performances; allocation of resources to particular roles; and role distancing behavior.[39]

Without pretending comprehensiveness, additional answers can also be suggested: evaluation of role performances, including self-evaluation, self-satisfaction, and the quality of role performance as reflected in objective rewards or in the evaluations of others; role "content" including the "style" in which a role is played (torpor, enthusiasm, etc.); adherence to institutionalized values or normative expectations; and visibility of role performances.

At this point, a set of hypotheses built on the basis of the preceeding discussion and conceptualization can be formu-

---

[38]It may be a useful reminder to note that by definition a role performance is interaction. Role behavior is social behavior.

[39]This term, taken from Goffman, refers to symbolic announcements that a role one is playing is not to be identified with the "real" person. See Erving Goffman, *Encounters,* (Indianapolis: Bobbs-Merrill, 1961), pp. 83–152.

lated. Intended to be only illustrative, the hypotheses offered are nevertheless clearly interdependent and taken together constitute an approximation of a theory proper. The hypotheses will be baldly stated without the full derivations that would serve to legitimate the set as a theory. To essay such derivations now would require more repetition of prior materials than is warranted.[40]

Hypothesis 1. The greater the commitment premised on an identity, the higher that identity will be in the salience hierarchy.

Hypothesis 2. The greater the commitment premised on an identity and the more positive the evaluation of that identity, the higher the identity will be in the salience hierarchy.

Hypothesis 3. The more a given network of commitment is premised on a particular identity as against other identities which may enter that network of commitment, the higher that identity will be in the salience hierarchy.

Hypothesis 4. The more congruent the role expectations of those to whom one is committed by virtue of a given identity, the higher that identity will be in the salience hierarchy.

Hypothesis 5. The larger the number of persons included in a network of commitment premised on a given identity for whom that identity is high in their own salience hierarchies, the higher that identity will be in the salience hierarchy.

Hypothesis 6. The higher an identity in the salience hierarchy, the greater the probability of role performances being consistent with the role expectations attached to that identity.

[40]The first of these hypotheses appear in Stryker, "Identity Salience and Role Performance," op. cit., and a somewhat more thorough rationale for them is available in that source.

Hypothesis 7. The higher an identity in the salience hierarchy, the greater the probability that a person will perceive a given situation as an opportunity to perform in terms of that identity.

Hypothesis 8. The higher an identity in the salience hierarchy, the greater the probability that a person will actively seek out opportunities to perform in terms of that identity.

Hypothesis 9. The greater the commitment, the higher the identity salience, the greater impact the quality of role performance will have on self-esteem.

Hypothesis 10. The greater the commitment, the higher the identity salience, the higher the probability that role performance will reflect institutionalized values and norms.

Hypothesis 11. External events cutting existing commitments will increase the probability of adoption of novel identities.

Hypothesis 12. The more that perceived consequences of a projected identity change are in the direction of reinforcing valued commitments, the less the resistance to change.

A Concluding Note

This chapter has presented one version of the symbolic interactionist framework. While not idiosyncratic, this version emphasizes social structure much more than most alternative versions; it tries to do more with social structure than assimilate it in the concept of definition of the situation or make it disappear entirely in the solvent of social process. This version, too, introduces a much more variegated conception of self in place of the unitary conception contained in some alternatives. Finally, while it has not been treated in this chapter, this version is much more compatible with conventional notions and methods of science than some alternatives; nothing in it prejudices the use of mathematical and statistical models and techniques of analysis, rigorous measurement procedures, or deductive theorizing.

Not all of the alternatives differ from the version presented in this chapter in all of these respects. Indeed, among the alternatives to be discussed in the following chapter are some which share in important degree the defining characteristics of the version presented. By the same token, of course, some differ considerably. That observation serves to move the discussion to a consideration of variants of the symbolic interactionist framework.

4

Contemporary Symbolic Interactionism: Variations

Introduction

Many who see themselves as working within the tradition of symbolic interactionism would not agree with everything in Chapter 3; at least a few would find virtually all of it objectionable; and some would argue that one or another element in the statement disqualifies it as being "genuinely" symbolic interactionism. Disputed elements might include: the interest in general theoretical propositions that can be tested through the derivation and empirical examination of hypotheses; the emphasis on the expectations of others as constraining actors' definitions of situations—their definitions of self, of others, and of remaining objects in the situation; the view of social structure as in part facilitating and in part constraining the choices made by human actors; the willingness to accept in principle the notion that symbolic interactionism may not be applicable to all of human behavior; and the stress on the potential usefulness of the full range of social science methods, including experimental procedures, mathematical and statistical modeling and estimation strategies, and measurement tactics designed to achieve comparative rigor and high reliability. Each of these characteristics of the statement will be read by at least some as being in violation of the spirit if not the logic of what they take to be truly symbolic interactionist.

As the foregoing suggests, there is no single symbolic interactionist orthodoxy. Instead, there is considerable variation in the ideas that are offered under that label. This chapter describes part of that variation through a review of the writings of a set of scholars whose work either has been in the recent past, is in the present, or is likely in the immediate future to be influential in shaping thinking about human interaction and its products, and who have been identified as working within the broad tradition of symbolic interactionism.

This last qualification implies that there are at least a few commonalities among symbolic interactionists. Describing what they take to be four distinct orientations within symbolic interactionism—a Chicago school, an Iowa school, the dramaturgical approach and ethnomethodology—Meltzer, Petras, and Reynolds[1] assert that each orientation accepts the premises that human beings act toward things on the basis of meanings those things have for them, that meanings are a product of social interaction, and that meanings are modified and handled through an interpretative process used by persons in dealing with things each encounters. A second attempt to delineate the core of symbolic interactionism does so in these terms:

> Humans create and use symbols. They communicate with symbols. They interact through role-taking, which involves the reading of symbols emitted by others. What makes them unique as a species—the existence of mind and self—arises out of interaction, while conversely, the emergence of these capacities allows for the interactions that form the basis of society.[2]

Still a third effort suggests a set of assumptions and a "predilection" as comprising the common elements that unite symbolic interactionists. According to this statement,[3] symbolic interactionists agree in the assumption that man must be studied on his own level and that reductionist efforts to infer valid principles of human behavior from the study of nonhuman forms are misguided. They agree that the most fruitful approach to man's social behavior is

[1]Meltzer, Petras, and Reynolds, op. cit., p. 54. These premises are taken from Blumer's characterization of the nature of symbolic interactionism in his essay on "The Methodological Position of Symbolic Interactionism." See Herbert Blumer, *Symbolic Interactionism: Perspective and Method* (Englewood Cliffs, N.J.: Prentice-Hall, 1969), pp. 2–6.

[2]Jonathan Turner, op. cit., pp. 329–330.

[3]Sheldon Stryker, "Symbolic Interaction as an Approach to Family Research," *Marriage and Family Living*, 31 (May, 1959):111–119.

through an analysis of society; that the human infant enters life as neither a social nor an antisocial creature with the potentialities for social development; and that the human being is an actor as well as a reactor. The predilection is to stay close to the world of everyday experience from which the viewpoint develops and with which it seeks to deal.

And, finally, Manis and Meltzer[4] offer the following as fundamental elements of symbolic interactionism:

1.   The meaning component in human conduct
2.   The social sources of humanness
3.   Society as process
4.   The voluntaristic component in human conduct
5.   A dialectical conception of mind
6.   The constructive, emergent nature of human conduct
7.   The necessity of sympathetic introspection[5]

There are differences within the commonality, however described, and the discussion now turns to these differences. No effort is made to represent all versions of symbolic interactionism. Apart from space limitations, the boundaries of that domain are simply not clear; for example, some would include ethnomethodology and various cognitive and phenomenological sociologies and some would not. The usual way of discussing variations within symbolic interactionism begins (and frequently ends) by distinguishing between Chicago and Iowa schools. This treatment remains true to this pattern by dealing with Herbert Blumer and Manford H. Kuhn, the major figures associated with the two schools.[6]

In important degree, the work of these two seminal interactionists now belongs in the past, a major effort of cur-

---

[4]Jerome G. Manis and Bernard N. Meltzer, *Symbolic Interaction* Third Edition (Boston: Allyn and Bacon, 1978), p. 5.

[5]Whether or not the necessity of sympathetic introspection can be accepted as a fundamental element of symbolic interactionism depends on whether it is intended as an exclusive methodological focus. Similarly, society as process is acceptable only if it does not entirely rule out a vision of society as structure. But these demurrers merely emphasize what has already been said: there is no single symbolic interactionist orthodoxy.

[6]Herbert Blumer spent most of his career at the University of Chicago, where he earned his Ph.D. in Sociology after working with Mead, Park, and Ellsworth Faris. He joined the faculty at Chicago in 1925 and remained there until 1952, when he moved to the University of California, Berkeley. Kuhn took his Ph.D. at the University of Wisconsin, working primarily with Kimball Young. He joined the faculty at the University of Iowa in 1946 and was on the faculty there at the time of his death in 1963.

rent symbolic interactionists (insofar as they do not simply repeat the dicta of their masters) being to transcend the antinomies implied by their writings. Since every current symbolic interactionist cannot be attended to, attention will focus on Ralph H. Turner, George J. McCall, Eugene Weinstein, and Peter J. Burke.[7] The principle underlying these choices is in keeping with the thrust of previous chapters which looked toward the development of a sound, researchable symbolic interactionist theory, argued the necessity of integrating social structural concepts into the traditional symbolic interactionist framework, and refused to rule out extant social science methods on the grounds of an assumed incompatibility with the nature of humans or the nature of society. Turner, McCall, Weinstein and Burke each accepts these "ground rules," though in varying degree. At the same time, again in varying degree, each emphasizes "the constructive, emergent nature of human conduct," "the voluntaristic component in human conduct," "society as process," the symbolic nature of human interaction, and the import of self in mediating social behavior. It is perhaps pertinent that Turner has been described as carrying on the tradition of Blumer, and McCall asserts his major intellectual debt to Kuhn.[8]

Herbert Blumer

Certainly the most influential voice since Mead in the elaboration of symbolic interactionism, a label he invented, Blumer stands in opposition to many of the assertions made in the name of that framework in the preceding pages.[9] Meltzer, Petras, and Reynolds argue that Blumer's methodological dicta are derived from his image of humans;[10]

[7]As earlier noted, this selection omits many contemporary symbolic interactionists whose work contains much of interest to any discussion of the significant variations in symbolic interactionism.

[8]George J. McCall and J. L. Simmons, *Identities and Interaction*, rev. ed., (New York: The Free Press, 1978), p. ix.

[9]Given this fact, it is clear that the writer can have little sympathy with stands that Blumer takes in his elaboration of symbolic interactionism. Every effort has been made to express Blumer's position fairly.

[10]They offer the opposite characterization of Kuhn, suggesting that the latter's methodology dictates his view of humans; and they obviously intend this as a derogatory comment. Whether either characterization is correct in fact cannot be known—both may be true, both may be false, one or the other may be true. whatever may be the case, for both Blumer and Kuhn there is a certain consistency between conceptual imagery and methodological preference; and it is convenient to treat the former as preceding the latter.

Hence, the discussion of Blumer's symbolic interactionism begins with his view of the human being and of the society human beings form, then moves to methodological matters.

In an essay entitled "Society as Symbolic Interaction,"[11] Blumer points to the "peculiar and distinctive character" of human interaction as the referent of symbolic interaction. The peculiarity, he notes, reflects the fact that humans do not simply react to one another's actions; rather, they interpret or define those actions. Their responses are based on meanings they attach to actions rather than the actions themselves. Human interaction is mediated by symbols, by interpretation, and by ascertaining the meaning of participants' actions.

Blumer credits Mead with having thought through what the act of interpretation implies for understanding the human being, human action, and human association. Mead, in saying that the human has a self, asserted that the human can be the object of his own actions. This ability to act toward oneself is the "central mechanism" in the human's dealings with the world: it enables one to indicate to oneself things in the world around and to guide actions by what is noted; and it creates objects, providing them with meaning. Instead of existing in the environment as stimuli, things in the world are given meaning by individuals. The human environment is a symbolic environment, constructed on the basis of ongoing activity. That humans make indications to themselves implies that their action is built-up instead of released (automatically triggered by a stimulus). Action is the product of the person's piecing together and guiding his own action by taking account of things and interpreting their significance for prospective action. Such construction of action through self-indication always takes place in a social context. Group action is the fitting together of individual lines of action, each person aligning his or her action to that of others through taking the role of the others, i.e., by seeking the meanings of their acts through ascertaining what they are doing or intend to do.

[11]Originally written for and published in Arnold M. Rose, ed., Human Behavior and Social Processes, (Boston: Houghton Mifflin, 1962). The essay reappears in Herbert Blumer, *Symbolic Interactionism* (Englewood Cliffs, N.J.: Prentice-Hall, 1969). Page references that follow are to the latter source; but, in general, specific page references are omitted.

These essential features in Mead's analysis of the bases of symbolic interaction, says Blumer, presuppose that society is made up of individuals who have selves; that individual action is a construction not a release; and that group or collective action consists of aligning individual actions through a process of individuals interpreting and taking into account one anothers' actions. And, he adds, "... the three premises can be easily verified empirically."

Arguing that, in general, sociological views of human society are at variance with these premises of symbolic interactionism, Blumer elaborates a conception of society he believes consistent with the premises. Society consists of acting people; the life of society consists of their actions. These actions take place in and with regard to a situation; they are constructed by interpreting the situation, by identifying the things that must be taken into account, assessing them, and making decisions on the basis of that assessment. This interpretative behavior takes place in individuals and in collectivities of individuals acting in concert, or when agents act on behalf of groups or organizations. "Group life consists of acting units developing acts to meet the situations in which they are placed."

Blumer recognizes that most situations encountered by members of a society are defined by them in the same way, through common understandings or definitions developed through previous interaction. He insists that even in such situations an interpretative process goes on through which the actions of participants are constructed. The fitting process organizing acts occurs with little strain when ready-made or commonly accepted definitions are available. When situations are not defined in a single way by participants, lines of action do not fit together readily and collective action is blocked. Then, interpretations have to be developed and worked out. There is an emerging process of definition which comes into play that must be caught by the student of society by examining the acting units that comprise society.

"Conventional" sociologists do not, contends Blumer, study human society in terms of its acting units. Rather, they view society as structure or organization and see action as an expression of this structure or organization, bypassing the acting units and the interpretative process through which action is built-up. The essential difference between conventional sociology and symbolic interaction is in the former's concern with organization and the latter's concern with acting units. For the former, organization is the determinant of action; for the latter, organization is only the framework within which social action takes place. Symbolic interactionism, according to Blumer, views social organization as entering action only to the extent that it shapes situations and provides fixed sets of symbols that people use in interpreting their situations. These influences are profound in settled and stabilized societies, but become less important in modern society where the increasing crisscrossing of lines of action means that situations arise for which there are no previously regularized and standardized actions. To the extent this occurs, social organization does not shape situations, and the symbols used by acting units may go beyond, or depart from, existing organization in its structural dimensions.

In Blumer's words:

> Students of human society will have to face the question of whether their preoccupation with categories of structure and organization can be squared with the interpretative process by which human beings, individually and collectively, act in human society. It is the discrepancy between the two which plagues such students in their efforts to attain scientific propositions of the sort achieved in the physical and biological sciences ... Efforts are made, of course, to overcome these shortcomings by devising new structural categories, by formulating new structural hypotheses, by developing more refined techniques of research, and even by formulating new methodological schemes of a structural character. These efforts continue to ignore or to explain away the interpretative process by which people act, individually and collectively, in society.[12]

In another essay,[13] Blumer makes clear his view that a sociological frame of reference that seeks to link social behavior to role requirements, situational demands, attitudes, motives, expectations, rules, etc., is inconsistent with the recognition that the human is a defining, interpreting, and

---

[12]Ibid., p. 89.
[13]"The Methodological Position of Symbolic Interactionism," op. cit. Again, specific page references will generally be omitted.

indicating creature. Such an approach, he argues, ignores and has no place for people with selves through which their worlds are handled and action constructed.

What holds for individual action holds for collective action, exemplified in the behavior of groups, institutions, organizations, and social classes. These consist of individuals fitting lines of action to one another, and so have the character of being constructed in situations through an interpretative process. This articulation of lines constitutes the social organization of conduct.

Failing to recognize that collective action is an interlinkage of separate acts of participants can lead to overlooking the fact that even well-established and repetitive forms of action have to be continuously formed anew through the process of interpretation and designation. Analysis of either change or stability in human society using concepts like culture, social order, norms, values, and rules, misses a basic point: "It is the social process in group life that creates and upholds the rules, not the rules that create and uphold group life." Further, the view of social organization and institutions as self-operating entities following their own dynamics and not requiring attention to participants within them is a serious mistake; social organization and institutions function because people at different points do something as the result of defining the situation in which they are called to act. And joint action arises out of the previous action of participants; it is an emergent from and is connected with that previous action. Thus joint action must always be understood in its historical context.

From this characterization of the nature of objects, human beings, and social life—a characterization which sees the environment, the person, and organized action as fluid, being continuously constructed and reconstructed and premised on definitional and interpretative processes—Blumer draws his methodological principles. The central principle is expressed in the form of an injunction: "Respect the nature of the empirical world and organize a methodological stance to reflect that respect."

Blumer's criticism of others' frames of reference for the study of social behavior is, fundamentally, that they do not meet the test of this principle. The empirical world is "obdurate," albeit not fixed or immutable. The empirical world is "real," but does not exist in some ultimate form awaiting discovery; it's reality is here and now, and is continuously recast in the light of new discoveries. Nor is the empirical world to be cast in terms of the findings of physical science; this, suggests Blumer, is an especially pernicious notion. Instead, empirical science requires that the prior pictures or schemes which are an unavoidable prerequisite for any study of the empirical world, the problems chosen to be pursued, the data selected and the means used to obtain the data, the connectives between the data, the interpretation of findings, and the concepts used—in brief, the essential aspects of the methodology of an empirical science—are all to be constructed *"in the light of the nature of the empirical world under study."* Each must be validated through the test of the empirical world. Adhering to a scientific protocol, engaging in replication of research, relying on the test of hypotheses, and employing operational procedures—the emphases of conventional methodology, according to Blumer—are no guarantees against operating with false premises, erroneous problems, distorted data, spurious relations, inaccurate concepts and unverified interpretations. The only assurances are to be found in direct, meticulous examination of the empirical world.

Blumer specifically does not mean to include as direct, meticulous examination of the empirical world, most of the work social scientists do. The use of census data, social surveys, questionnaires, polls, scales, refined measuring instruments, experimental studies, computer simulation and "crucial empirical data to test hypotheses" are abjured as militating against the direct examination being called for.

The empirical social world in the case of human beings is what they actually experience and do. It includes individual activities and the interlaced activities of many individuals. It is the world of everyday experience, the "top layers" of which we see in our own and others' lives. Ongoing group life is the empirical social world of the social and psychological sciences and the methodological problem is to become acquainted with it on a firsthand basis; for, in the absence of such acquaintance, preestablished images control inquiry. Rather than being tested and modified by a firsthand acquaintance with a sphere of life, these images become a substitute for that acquaintance.

Given that one typically does not have firsthand knowledge to begin with, and given that there is a persistent tendency for humans to build separate social worlds, how does one get close enough to the empirical social world to dig deeply into it? Doing so, says Blumer, is more than just looking; it is a tough task requiring disciplined imagination, resourcefulness, flexibility, pondering over what one sees, and a constant readiness to reshape one's views and guiding images. It involves two modes of inquiry which Blumer terms "exploration" and "inspection."

Exploration is by definition a flexible procedure not pinned to any particular technique. It begins with broad focus but narrows progressively as the investigator moves toward an understanding of how the problem is to be posed, what the appropriate data may be, what conceptual tools may be useful, etc. Exploration differs from the "pretentious posture" of working with established scientific protocol which requires the researcher to know in advance, precisely what the problem is and what kinds of data are to be collected; to have a prearranged set of techniques; and to use established conceptual categories.

The guiding maxim of exploration is to use any ethical procedure, with the possibility of providing a clearer picture of what may be going on in an area of social life. It may involve observation, interviewing, listening to conversations, obtaining life histories, using letters and diaries, arranging for group discussions, and consulting public records. Participants should be sought out who are, in the sphere of life under study, acute, well-informed observers. Blumer suggests that a small number of such persons brought together in a discussion and resource group, will be more useful than any other means to illuminate the sphere of life, and "more valuable many times over than any representative sample."

During exploration, the researcher constantly tests and revises images, beliefs, and conceptions of the social world being studied, doing so through direct observation but also by posing questions that sensitize the observer to different and new perspectives, and by recording observations that challenge working conceptions or those that are simply odd and interesting but whose relevance is not clear.

Sometimes such exploration will answer theoretical

questions a scholar has in mind without invoking a theory or analytic scheme. But exploration does not exhaust what is required by direct examination of the empirical world. The construction of a comprehensive and intimate account of what takes place in the empirical social world should be followed by analysis. Scientific analysis requires clear, discriminating, analytic elements and the isolation of relationships between these elements. The procedure through which these requirements are met is inspection.

Analysis involves casting a problem in theoretical form, unearthing generic relations, sharpening the connotative reference of concepts, and formulating theoretical propositions. Blumer rejects what he calls the scheme of scientific analysis espoused in current methology which he describes as starting with a theory or model framed in terms of relationships between concepts, using the theory to set up a specific problem, converting the problem into independent and dependent variables representing concepts, employing precise techniques to obtain data, discovering relations between variables, and using the theory or model to explain these relations. Inspection, as an alternative, involves a close, shifting scrutiny of whatever analytic elements are used for analysis (e.g., integration or mobility); it involves looking at the empirical instances covered by a given analytic element in a variety of different ways, viewing them from different angles, and scrutinizing them from the standpoint of many different questions. Inspection is flexible, imaginative, creative, and free to take new directions. It is not preset, routinized, nor prescribed. It is the antithesis of conventional current methodology.

The basic premises of symbolic interactionism must have their empirical validity tested, but they cannot be tested by what Blumer calls the "alien criteria of an irrelevant methodology," i.e., by conventional methods. Instead, "they can be readily tested and validated merely by observing what goes on in social life under one's nose."[14]

Given that the premises of symbolic interactionism are validated, suggests Blumer, certain methodological implications follow. That people act on the basis of the meaning of their objects implies that to understand their actions it is

14Ibid., pp. 49–50.

necessary to see their objects as they see them. One must have descriptive accounts from the actors in a situation of how they see and act toward objects; such descriptive accounts are rarely yielded by standard research procedure. In order to guard against deficiencies, the depiction of key objects in individual accounts should be subject to probing and critical discussion by a group of well-informed participants in a given social world. And the assumption that one sees objects as others see them, must be avoided.

From the premise that group life is a process in which individuals build their lines of action by interpreting and taking into account one another's actions, follows the implication that social interaction cannot be treated merely as the medium through which determining factors produce behavior; interaction must be seen as a formative process in its own right. Nor can interaction be compressed into any special form, whether as a process of developing complimentary expectations,[15] or as conflict, or in game-theoretic terms. Interaction is diverse; the form it does take is a matter of empirical discovery rather than something fixed in advance.

The view of social action as being constructed through an interpretative process has, as a methodological consequence, the requirement that the process of construction be observed in order to analyze social action. This cannot be done on the premise that social action is the product of preexisting causative factors. The formation of action must be traced by seeing the situation as it is seen by the actor, observing what the actor takes into account and how he interprets what is taken, noting alternative acts that are mapped out, and trying to follow the interpretation that leads to the selection of one of these acts.

Finally, Blumer contends that the study of a complex organization or complexly organized area of social life poses no methodological problem any different from those posed in the study of an individual's lines of actions.

Repeated reference has been made to Blumer's criticisms of the conceptual and methodological positions taken by others. Blumer defines his own position largely in contrast

[15]This notion, central to the theory of Talcott Parsons, is termed "quaint" by Blumer. Ibid., p. 53.

to sociology as it is generally practiced. Brief discussions of two of his more important critical essays will perhaps help to further delineate his position.

"What is Wrong with Social Theory,"[16] develops a distinction between "definitive concepts" and "sensitizing concepts." Blumer argues that the crux of the problem of social theory—its divorcement from the empirical world, its inability to guide research, its failure to benefit from accumulated results of empirical observation and research—lies in the nature of its concepts. Concepts link theory to the empirical world; but the concepts are distressingly vague, and this ambiguity is the basic deficiency in social theory. Attempts to resolve ambiguity through developing fixed and specific procedures, in order to isolate a stable and definitive empirical content, have failed. But this failure aside, the question of whether definitive concepts are suited to the study of the empirical social world, makes such efforts inherently problematic. A definitive concept refers precisely to what is common to a class of objects through a clear definition in terms of attributes or fixed bench marks. The natural social world of everyday experience, the empirical world of sociology, consists of objects each of which has a distinctive, peculiar or unique character which must be included in our handling of these objects. That being the case, definitive concepts cannot be formed. Instead, we must form sensitizing concepts that give a user only general guidance to the empirical world. "Whereas definitive concepts provide prescriptions of what to see, sensitizing concepts merely suggest directions along which to look." Clearly, this emphasis on sensitizing concepts fits well with Blumer's vision of the tentative, changeable nature of social action and with the methodological canons discussed above.

"Sociological Analysis and the 'Variable',"[17] details Blumer's discontent with developments in sociology through a

[16]Herbert Blumer, "What is Wrong with Social Theory," *American Sociological Review,* 19 (February, 1954):3–10. Reprinted in Herbert Blumer, *Symbolic Interactionism,* op. cit.

[17]Herbert Blumer, "Sociological Analysis and the 'Variable' " *American Sociological Review,* 22 (December, 1956):683–690. Reprinted in Herbert Blumer, *Symbolic Interactionism,* op. cit., pp. 127–139.

critical examination of what he calls "variable analysis," a scheme which "reduces" social life to variables and their relations. In use, variable analysis is said to have a number of shortcomings: there are no rules, guides, limitations or prohibitions governing the choice of variables; there are none or few generic variables (those standing for abstract categories) without which analysis yields only disconnected findings; and data and findings in variable analyses are of the here and now, yet—being a single relation between two variables—they are barren of context necessary to understanding a here and now relationship.

But the basic question is whether variable analysis is suited to the study of human group life, suggests Blumer, and his answer is "no." The process of interpretation or definition intrinsic to human groups sets a crucial limit to the application of variable analysis. When variable analysis deals with areas of group life involving interpretation, it is disposed to ignore the process. It does so by assuming that an independent variable automatically affects a dependent variable, a fallacy based on the tacit, further assumption that the former predetermines its interpretation. That assumption has no foundation: "Since anything that is defined may be redefined, the relation has no intrinsic fixity." Interpretations have varying and shifting content, and cannot be given the qualitative constancy required of a variable. Thus this central feature of individual and group experience cannot be captured within the logic of variable analysis. Further, the "true" sociological variable has no empirical reference which is either unitary or distinct, characteristics required by the logic of variable analysis. The actual social character of empirical references is complex and "inner-moving," and so fails to meet these requirements. Consequently, variable analyses gloss over the character of the real operating factors in group life and the real interaction and relations between such factors.

Manford H. Kuhn

Blumer's symbolic interactionism received relatively full treatment in these pages because it stands in sharp contrast with the statement of the position presented in Chapter 3.

Kuhn's symbolic interactionism can be treated more briefly, in part because it is essentially (though not completely) consonant with that statement.[18]

Kuhn's version of symbolic interactionism focuses on the concepts of self and of role-taking.[19] Indeed, he chose the label "self-theory" to describe that version, doing so, however, not for conceptual reasons but to emphasize an interest in developing generalizations tested by empirical research, in contrast to what he saw as the conjectural and deductive orientation in the work of Cooley, Dewey, and Mead. Theoretically and conceptually, he regarded his symbolic interactionism as "orthodox," and as derivative of the writings of those founding fathers. And, while he clearly had his preferences, he by no means regarded his preferences as exclusionary; rather, he assimilates a wide range of materials to symbolic interactionism. In particular he assimilates role theory (which he suggests is hardly if at all distinguishable from symbolic interactionism) and reference group theory.

That Kuhn characterizes the relation between symbolic interactionism and role theory as he does, speaks to his view of both the character and the relevance of social structure or social organization. Social structure is seen as consisting of networks of positions and the roles (expectations) that accompany those positions. He assesses role theoretic research by suggesting that "it has underscored Thomas' dictum that 'people tend to play the roles assigned to them.' " Accepting the view that social structure is created, maintained, and altered through symbolic interaction, he also regards social structure—once created—as constraining interaction.

Nevertheless, there are clearly cautionary notes in his identification of role theory and symbolic interactionism. The emphasis of the former, he notes, is on overt role-play-

[18]For explicit, extensive and helpful comparative treatments of Blumer and Kuhn, see Meltzer, Petras, and Reynolds, op. cit., and Jonathan Turner, op. cit.

[19]These emphases were at the core of Kuhn's own work and that of his students at the University of Iowa. It would appear that they were deliberately selected to follow the programmatic proposals regarding needed work in social psychology by Leonard S. Cottrell, Jr. in his presidential address to the American Sociological Society, published as "Some Neglected Problems in Social Psychology," *American Sociological Review,* 15 (December, 1950):705–712. See Manford H. Kuhn, "Major Trends in Symbolic Interaction Theory in the Past Twenty-Five Years," *The Sociological Quarterly,* 5 (Winter, 1964):61–84.

ing and on the relation of role performances to role expectations; and there is little or no emphasis on role-taking, the
"interior" process of the self, or self-sentiments. Role theory, he recognizes along with Ralph Turner, tends toward
the processes of conformity. Also, in commenting on the
implications of role-theoretic research findings, he suggests
that strong evidence of a totally determinate relationship
between role expectations and role performances does not
exist, but that knowledge of expectations does permit one to
use probabilistic predictions with respect to behaviors.

Insofar as Kuhn sees a strong determinancy in social life,
he tends to see it in the relationship of self to behavior. His
review of developments in symbolic interactionism over
the twenty-five year period from 1937–1962, begins by noting the considerable ambiguity and contradictions in
Mead's writing with regard to the fact and location of determinancy or indeterminancy in the relation of society to self
and self to behavior. Distinguishing between various types
of determinate and indeterminate symbolic interactionist
theory, he locates his own and his students' work among the
former:

> ... self theory ... has implied one or another of the five deter-
> minate models ... although this point is implicit rather than
> explicit, and never a salient issue. The general attempt rests
> on the notion that there is among the several important mat-
> ters a procedure considered nomothetic or genotypical by the
> symbolic interaction orientation.[20]

Self-theory obviously requires a conception of self. Again,
Kuhn begins with Mead's view of humans as capable of
responding to themselves as objects, through their capacity
to create and to use symbols. Objects for Mead are plans of
action, he notes, and that notion equates with Mead's conception of an attitude.[21] Kuhn suggests that considerable
conceptual clarification results from the conscious conceptualization of the self as a set of attitudes, a conceptualization consistent with Mead's view that the self is an object in

[20]Ibid., p. 72.
[21]One sees the meaning of this assertion in Mead's phrase "take the attitude of
the other," which he used as an alternative formulation to "take the role of the
other." As earlier stressed, role-taking (or attitude-taking) involves the anticipation of the future actions or behavior of another; thus the equation of attitude and
"plan of action."

most respects like any other object, and with his view that an object is a plan of action.[22]

For Kuhn, the concept of self embodies an approach to personality consistent with the assumptions and findings of social science. The social science view, he says, is that people organize and direct their behaviors in terms of their subjectively defined identifications. These are the internalizations of the objective social statuses persons occupy, but in a secular society there is a looseness between social systems and the individual occupants of statuses in them—there are alternatives, change, and collective behavior. Consequently, in order to predict how people organize and direct their behavior, the subjective definitions of identity are required. In this sense, the most significant object to be defined in a stituation is the self. As Kuhn writes:

> As self theory views the individual, he derives his plans of action from the roles he plays and the statuses he occupies in the groups with which he feels identified—his reference groups. His attitudes toward himself as an object are the best indexes to these plans of action, and hence to action itself, in that they are the anchoring points from which self-evaluations are made.[23]

Kuhn's theorizing gives an important place to a "core self," a stable set of meanings attached to oneself as an object. A core self is both the product of the expectations of groups in which the person interacts and a shaper of interaction. It serves to constrain definitions of the situations, cues to which persons react, and objects that enter interaction. A core self provides structure and comparative stability to personality, and gives continuity and predictability to behavior.[24]

At the same time, the self is visualized as a structure of components. Kuhn conceptualizes self-definitions as com-

[22]Manford H. Kuhn and Thomas S. McPartland, "An Empirical Investigation of Self-Attitudes," *American Sociological Review,* 19 (February, 1954):68.

[23]Hickman and Kuhn, op. cit., p. 45.

[24]See C. Addison Hickman and Manford H. Kuhn, *Individuals, Groups, and Economic Behavior.* (New York: Dryden, 1956), esp. pp. 21–45; Manford H. Kuhn, "Family Impact on Personality," in J. E. Hulett and R. Stagner, *Problems in Social Psychology* (Urbana: University of Illinois Press, 1953); Manford H. Kuhn, "Factors in Personality: Socio-Cultural Determinants as Seen Through the Amish," in Francis L. Kittsu, ed., *Aspects of Culture and Personality,* (New York: Abelard-Schuman, 1954).

posed of consensual and subconsensual references; the former "refer to groups and classes whose conditions of membership and limits are matters of common knowledge," the latter "to groups, classes, attributes, traits or any other matters which would require interpretation by the respondent to be precise or to place him relative to other people." Examples of the former include student, girl, husband; examples of the latter include happy, interesting, good wife, heavy. And he recognized variation in salience both between and within these categories; in brief, he saw self-attitudes as hierarchized.

He also argued the need to go beyond subjective identifications in status terms to fully discover the self and realized the need to know roles, role preferences, role avoidances, role expectations, areas of self-threat and vulnerability, self-enhancing evaluations, patterns of reference group selections including negative as well as positive others, and "probably" self-dissociated attitudes. Given the complexity of the self when these various segments are put together, Kuhn clearly does not anticipate any simple connective between self and behavior, and his framework does not lack the conceptual means to begin tracing out the variety of connectives.

If the core self constrains interaction, there is clearly less room for creativity and innovation than there would otherwise be. Thus, as a function of the stability of the self, there is also stability in interaction. Much interaction, in Kuhn's view, simply follows the expectations that impinge on participants from one another. Again, however, this emphasis on stability is only relative. Some potential for volatility is introduced by recognizing the "slippage" between social structure and self-attitudes, and there is some potential for creativity through the role-taking process. Along with symbolic interactionists in general, Kuhn notes that actors can use the perspectives of others as a basis for adjusting and controlling their own responses—and, given multiple other perspectives, this can mean that the direction taken by self control may be away from simply meeting the expectations of others.

Conceptualizations of self, interaction, and social structure as relatively stable and not continuously shifting, suggests the possibility of reliable measurement. Kuhn's methodological thrust is toward conventional science. He seeks general propositions from which specific hypotheses can be deduced and tested, the end result being a theory that can predict and explain human behavior and interaction. The strategy for developing such a theory is through the utilization of concepts of a tentative theoretical statement in empirical research; and the key to the successful use of concepts in research is proper measurement.

The starting point of proper measurement is precise specification of theoretical concepts. Kuhn sees no contradiction between the kind of concepts symbolic interactionism entails—concepts that refer to meanings, to the internal and subjective, to symbolic processes—and meeting conventional scientific criteria for standardized, objective, dependable measures. He calls for these measures; he anticipates the accelerated development of such measures; and in these terms he sees the contribution that he and his students have made to symbolic interactionism.

Kuhn's work on measuring the self provides an example of how his programmatic aspirations were to be fulfilled. Noting that while the self has been the central concept of symbolic interactionism, little work using it in empirical research had been done.[25] Kuhn attributes this largely to the absence of consensus with regard to the class of phenomena to which the concept ought be operationally ordered; and he proposes a remedy through conceptualizing the self as a set of attitudes. If, as he argues, human behavior is organized and directed, and if the organization and direction are supplied by persons' attitudes toward themselves, it becomes of crucial significance to identify and measure self-attitudes.

To this end, Kuhn—along with his student McPartland—attempted to construct and standardize a test to identify and measure self-attitudes. The product of this effort was the Twenty Statements Test, which asked persons to respond to the question "Who am I?" with twenty different answers. Responses were content analyzed, subjected to scaling procedures, and examined for validity using the "known groups" technique. Subsequently, the test developed through this procedure was examined for its reliability, and

---

[25]The time referent for this assertion is 1954.

used in dozens of researches in the effort to examine hypotheses formulated in terms of a symbolic interactionist framework.[26]

Ralph H. Turner

As Jonathan Turner notes,[27] for over two decades Ralph H. Turner has offered a consistent set of criticisms of role theory. He has used these criticisms as the starting point of a theoretical effort synthesizing symbolic interactionist and role theoretic elements in "something akin to axiomatic theory,"[28] a set of general propositions from which more specific propositions follow. Given the verification in empirical research of hypotheses drawn from the specific propositions, the general propositions can be said to explain the more specific propositions and empirical findings.

A major criticism of role theory made by Turner, one shared by virtually all whose theoretical thought has been influenced by symbolic interactionism, is that it has an overly structured view of human behavior, both personal and social.[29] Role theory seems to visualize behavior as simply the enactment of a script provided by normative expectations. There is little room in this vision for departures from that script except as "abnormal" social processes which generate correctives moving toward restoring prior balances and which change basic social structure only if they—so to speak—get out of hand. Turner does not deny the

[26]Tucker, in a detailed critique of Kuhn's theoretical and methodological work, argues that Kuhn's methodology and the Twenty Statements Test (TST) can be equated; and Meltzer, Petras, and Reynolds accept this characterization. See C. W. Tucker, "Some Methodological Problems of Kuhn's Self Theory," *Sociological Quarterly,* 7 (Summer, 1966) 345–358; and Meltzer, Petras, and Reynolds, op. cit., p. 59. Since it turns out that the TST does indeed have its problems and is not particularly reliable, the equation of this measure with Kuhn's methodology conveniently serves to discredit the latter. There is little fairness and less logic in this. The methodological principles for which Kuhn argued do not stand or fall on the basis of any particular measurement effort. For a comprehensive review of the TST in its various versions, its reliability and its research utilization, see Steven Spitzer, Carl J. Couch, and John R. Stratton, *The Assessment of Self* (Iowa City, Iowa: Escort-Sernoll, no date).

[27]Jonathan Turner, op. cit., p. 370. This section makes considerable use of Jonathan Turner's excellent review and synopsis of Ralph H. Turner's theoretical work.

[28]Ralph H. Turner, "A Strategy for Developing an Integrated Role Theory," unpublished paper.

[29]Ralph H. Turner, "Role-Taking: Process versus Conformity," in Arnold M. Rose, ed., *Human Behavior and Social Processes* (Boston: Houghton Mifflin, 1962).

applicability of what he calls this "conformity model"; his argument is that not all empirical situations can be accounted for in terms of actors perceiving normative expectations attaching to the positions they occupy, enacting behavior in conformity to those expectations, and being rewarded via social approval for that conforming behavior. Closely related is a second criticism: role theory tends to ignore the normal processes of social interaction in its focus on role strain and role conflict.

A third major criticism made by Turner concerns the status of role theory qua theory. Rather than unified and interrelated, its propositions have little connection with one another. This state of affairs relates to the absence of any reasonable consensus with respect to the meaning of "role."[30] That term has, variously, referred to expected behaviors, conceptions of expected behaviors, behavior one learns to play in specific situations, overt behavior of persons, and norms attached to statuses or positions. Turner argues not for a focus on one of these as the true focus of the concept, but the incorporation of all facets into a unified conception of role. Through this unified conception, he hopes to be able to analyze the interactive processes underlying the creation and maintenance of, and changes in, patterns of social organization.

Turner's last major criticism of role theory is that it fails to make adequate use of Mead's concept of role-taking. Making that concept central to theoretical thinking is, for Turner, a key to the development of a theory which at the same time can handle both stable, structured forms of social organization and less structured, fluid forms as well, and can deal with the full range of cooperation through conflictful social processes.

Turner seeks to remake role theory by bringing to it an appreciation for the role-taking concept and by using that concept as a corrective for its overly structured and conformist quality.[31] He regards role-taking as the core process

[30]Ralph H. Turner, "Social Roles: Sociological Aspects," in David L. Sills, ed., *International Encyclopedia of the Social Sciences* (New York: Macmillan, 1968).
[31]The point could have been stated the other way around i.e., to suggest that Turner seeks to remake symbolic interactionism by bringing to it an appreciation for social structure. It is stated as it is because Turner writes of developing a role theory.

in interaction, and asserts that it is the tendency to shape the phenomenal world into roles which is the key to role-taking. Role-taking is seen in Mead's terms, as a process of putting oneself in another's place and adjusting behavior accordingly in the course of interaction through the use of significant symbols. These symbols—words, inflections, expressions, dress—act as cues to the other's future behavior.

Turner argues that humans act as if others in the situations they meet are playing identifiable roles, and they role-take in order to identify those roles. The assumption that others are playing identifiable roles provides a common basis for interaction. Gestures and cues are read to ascertain what these roles are. Persons role-take in order to make sense of the other's actions and to facilitate their own responses to the other. But cultural definitions of roles are often vague and contradictory; consequently, cultural definitions provide at best a very general framework within which one can construct his or her own lines of action. That being the case, actors will have to make their roles and then communicate to others what roles they are playing.[32]

Thus, people do not simply enact roles; they make or create roles. They do so in order to fill out the loose cultural framework within which they act; they do so because they search for underlying roles in others' and their own behaviors in order to make sense of those behaviors; and they do so in order to be able to communicate with others the roles they are playing. In brief, they do so to enable and to facilitate interaction with others.

The notion of role-making emphasizes the tentative nature of interaction. So viewed, interaction involves continuously testing the conception one has of the role of the other. One will act as though the other is in a particular role as long as the assumption works, as long as it provides a stable and effective framework for interaction.

Thus, persons in interaction will continuously assess one another's behavior to see whether that behavior and associated cues "verify" or "validate" the occupancy of a position and the playing of a role. If another's behavior can be seen as a coherent whole, interaction with that other will be

[32]Ralph H. Turner, "Role-Taking as Process" and "Role-Playing and Process," unpublished papers.

facilitated because if one can make sense of another's behavior, one can anticipate that other's responses. If responses are not consistent, they cannot be seen as part of an underlying role, thus, interacting with that other will be problematic. Consistency permits an actor to discern roles to be played; consequently, persons' interactions with one another are based on an implicit norm of consistency.

The roles inferred on the basis of consistency are subject to verification or validation through the application of external and internal criteria. The internal criterion most frequently used is whether the actor sees the inferred role as facilitating interaction. The external criteria involve the probability that the role one infers would also be inferred by others and relevant groups, or inferred on the basis of commonly agreed upon standards. Validated or verified roles are the stable bases for interaction.

On the one hand, then, Turner emphasizes the role concept, albeit in a modified form. On the other hand, his emphasis is on self, which is in keeping with his fundamental symbolic interactionism. Humans' self-responses emerge out of their interaction with others, and humans present themselves to others in terms of their self-conceptions. As an actor seeks to infer the role of the other, so the other seeks to infer the role of the actor. The actor will then seek to inform the other through vocal and other behavioral gestures of the role being played. The actor will also seek to convey information about his or her self, about the degree to which roles being played are consistent with images of self; the self is invested in a role, and self and role "merge."[33] The actor will do so because self-presentations are attempts to reinforce self-conceptions.

The foregoing reviews Turner's efforts to correct the first three of his four major criticisms of role theory. It also "solves" the problem of the disparate meanings of role by emphasizing the processual nature of roles without sacrificing a reasonable structural view. As Jonathan Turner writes:

> ... the emphasis on behavioral aspect of role is retained, since it is through behavioral cues that actors impute roles.

[33]Ralph H. Turner, "The Role and the Person," *American Journal of Sociology,* 84 (July, 1978):1–23.

The notion that roles are conceptions of expected behaviors is preserved, for the assignment of a role to a person invokes an expectation that a certain type and range of responses will ensue. The view that roles are norms attendant on status positions is not ignored, since norms and positions are often the basis for assigning and verifying roles. And the conception of roles as parts that people learn to play is preserved, for people are able to denote each other's roles by virtue of their prior socialization into a common role repertoire ... These assumptions also point to the normal processes of interaction, but are sufficiently general to embrace the possibility of conflictful and stressful interactions. And these assumptions about the role-making process do not preclude the analysis of structured interaction, since formal norms and status positions are often the major cues for ascertaining the roles of people, while being the principle sources of verification for ascertaining their roles.[34]

Turner's fourth criticism of role theory, that it consists of disparate and unrelated propositions, is to be met using a strategy for theory building that seeks unifying themes linking various role processes.[35] He urges one to begin with sensitizing concepts and with narrow propositions and hypotheses in the research literature and move to precise definitions and to more general, formal theoretical propositions. One looks for propositions that link concepts to empirical regularities and that express the major tendencies of those regularities; an example is provided below. Then one looks for variables that act as determinants of variation in those regularities and groups related regularities together. Finally, one asks whether there may be some common principle that could explain why the groupings of regularities should occur. Two explanatory propositions have been offered: roles are used to achieve ends efficiently; and, the playing of roles is a means of achieving personal reward—validation of self, reinforcement from others, self-esteem, etc.

This strategy of theory building is seen in Turner's treatment of the role-person merger, the extent to which attitudes and behavior expressing one role carry over into other situations.[36] Conceptualizing the person as consisting of all

[34]Ibid., p. 374.
[35]Ralph H. Turner, "A Strategy for Developing an Integrated Role Theory," unpublished paper.
[36]Ralph H. Turner, "The Role and the Person," op. cit.

the roles in an individual's repertoire and noting that these repertoires are organized into hierarchies, he suggests that the person is best described in terms of the roles that are played when not called for and that affect the way other roles are played. And he notes that this way of viewing the person relates more meaningfully to social structure.

Turner offers three principal criteria of role-person merger: playing a role in situations where it does not apply; resisting the abandonment of a role despite viable and advantageous alternatives; acquiring attitudes and beliefs appropriate to a role.[37] At this point, he raises the question of the determinants of mergers and outlines two types, interactive and individual. With respect to each he then asks what functions are served for those interacting by the concept of person. Conceiving of another with whom one interacts as a person, i.e. as playing roles, is useful because it helps to answer these questions: will the allocation of roles in an interactive episode carry over to successive episodes; can actors be depended upon to carry out the implied and expressed commitments of their roles; which role (when the other is viewed as holding different roles in various settings) will govern the other's orientation when boundaries between settings are loose; and what role will govern when situations are undefined? As these questions imply, "the concept of the person is shaped ... in the service of social control," for effective and lasting social control "requires a less ephemeral object than the actor playing a particular role."[38]

These interactive functions of the role-person merger lead to three guiding interactive principles: (1) an *appearance principle* stating that in the absence of contradictory cues, people tend to accept others as they appear; (2) an *effect principle* stating that the disposition to see people on the basis of their role behavior will vary directly with the potential effect of the role on interaction; and (3) a *consistency principle,* stating that people, in the absence of strong contradictory indications, are disposed to accept the least complicated view of the person that facilitates interaction.

---

[37]Ibid., pp. 3–4. The relationship of role-person merger to the concept of identity salience, measured in terms of the probability of invoking an identity across situations, offered in Chapter 3, is clear.

[38]Ibid., p. 5.

At this point, again, propositions emerging from the guiding principles are offered. Illustratively, from the appearance principle comes the proposition that the more inflexible the allocation of actors to the role, the greater the tendency for members of the social circle to conceive of the person as revealed by the role. The effect principle leads to, among others, the proposition that the greater the potential power or the discretion vested in a role, the greater the tendency for members of the social circle to conceive the person as revealed by the role, and so on.

The individual functions of role-person merger include establishing a basis for understanding, predicting, and controlling others by becoming reasonably understandable and predictable to them;[39] economizing effort when playing many roles; facilitating control and autonomy (in the absence of a trans-situational anchorage, Turner argues, the actor is strictly a creature of each situation and associated roles); enabling the individual to maximize favorable interaction by continuing to play roles providing gratification, and obtaining rewards commensurate with investments made in particular roles.

Three guiding principles consistent with these functions are offered: a *consensual frame of reference principle* suggesting that individuals tend to merge into their persons those roles by which significant others identify them; an *autonomy and favorable-evaluation principle* saying that selective merger of roles into person will occur in order to maximize autonomy and self-evaluation; and an *investment principle,* asserting that individuals will merge into their persons those roles in which investment has been greatest or in which adequate return for investment is yet to come.

And, again, propositions are inferred from principles: for example, the more intensely and consistently that significant others identify a person on the basis of a certain role, the greater the tendency for individuals to merge the role and especially positively-evaluated roles, with their person.

Turner introduces social structure into his theorizing in important ways other than through the concepts of position

[39]Turner argues that it is a paradox of interaction that one must be reasonably comprehensible and predictable to others if one is to understand, predict, and control these others; and that the easiest way to be comprehensible to others is to be the person they have constructed. Ibid., p. 12.

and normative expectations per se. That is, while his work begins with a critique of role theory as overly structured, he retains a view of larger social structure as both constraining the self and social interaction, and as the product of self and interaction. Thus, in the essay on role-person merger, he suggests that roles tied to broad institutional sectors, such as family and occupational roles, will more often be seen as clues to the person than will roles held in narrow, little-known organizations. He notes that the community will organize relationships and bring social circles together or segregate them; this, in turn, will critically affect role-person merger. He observes that some principles governing role-person merger deriving from individual and interactive functions do not articulate and that while individual and interactional processes often converge in their operation, they sometimes fail to do so; an example is the frequent rejection by individuals of the community's presumption that the wife-mother role most fully shows the woman as a person. He relates such discrepancies to the segregation of social circles,[40] to social movements, to societal complexity, and to looseness in the organization of society. And he adds that one way of resolving the disjunct between community attributions of role to person and personal organization, may be to remain uninvolved in one's institutional roles.

The implications of involvement or lack thereof in institutional roles is further developed in an essay on the "real self."[41] By "real self" Turner means not some objectively determined "true" person, but a subjectively held sense which people have of who and what they really are. The articulation of real selves with social structure, he proposes, should be a major link in the functioning and change of societies, and it represents an approach to the relation of person and social structure that is especially compatible with symbolic interactionism as a perspective stressing the ongoing creation of reality by each member of society.

Self as object can have an institutional focus or it can be identified as strictly impulse. In varying degree, people will

[40]His term, social circles, appears to mean what others mean by the terms groups and social networks.

[41]Ralph H. Turner, "The Real Self: From Institution to Impulse," *American Journal of Sociology*, 81 (March, 1976):989–1016.

accept as evidence of their real selves, feelings, attitudes, and actions anchored in institutions: the self is recognized in acts of volition and in the pursuit of institutionalized goals; the true self is seen in action through acceptance of group obligations and strong loyalty to social forms. Alternatively, and again in varying degree, people take angry outburst or a sense that they are expressing deep, unsocialized, untamed impulse as being their actual selves; they play the institutional game when they have to, but feel that doing so is at the expense of the true self.

Turner's speculative hypothesis is that the past several decades have witnessed substantial shifts in the locus of self from an institutional to an impulse emphasis (in American society only; Turner does not presume the conceptual distinction valid for all societies). And he proposes a variety of possible theories and explanations of self-loci that seek to combine insights about individual dynamics and about social structure and culture. For present purposes, however, interest lies in what he has to say about shifts in the locus of self and what they imply for social structure.

The consequences of any massive shift should be substantial, he suggests. Sociological theories rooted in the past take for granted an actor who locates his real self in the institutional setting.[42] They see pathology as the result, when institutional participation is based on instrumental motivation and when only impulses that seem unrelated to institutions are taken to be genuine. The alternate loci of self bear importantly on social control through the phenomena of role distance, values and norms, sentiments, and ritual. In Turner's words:

> Concern with the prestige of one's role and the esteem that goes with high role adequacy buttresses the institutional structure. A sense of value eases the pathos of conformity with social norms. Social sentiments domesticate potentially disruptive emotions yet preserve their sensed vitality and spontaneity. And through collective ritual, group solidarity and dedication to the institutional structure are continually renewed. But all of this depends on the individual's feelings

[42]This is, he says, no less true for conflict theories than for order theories, the former simply shifting the locus of self to a class-bound institutional framework. Ibid., p. 1007.

that his real self is engaged in these experiences. If he finds that self elsewhere, control can only be instrumental.[43]

The most serious implication for social structure, Turner suggests, is contained in a hypothesized correlation between self-locus and a disposition to perceive either values or norms. Sociologists tend to reify the distinction, to write as though these were distinctive entitites in society. Instead, he argues, the nature of self-conception and the way self-conception identifies the relation of the individual to society leads persons to perceive, principally, values or norms. Perceiving values and discovering the real self in the performance of institutional roles facilitate social control systems as described in the extant sociological literature. Perceiving norms and recognizing the real self in impulse outside of any institutional bases introduce a very different system of social control, one not yet well described in the sociological literature.

George J. McCall

The major statement of George J. McCall's version[44] of symbolic interactionism[45] begins with an acknowledgment of indebtedness to Manford Kuhn, and recognition that Kuhn would not subscribe to all that is said in that work. Turner began with Blumer and found it necessary to move towards

[43]Ibid., p. 1011. Turner does not hold that persons whose real self is located in impulse are outside the process of social control, only that these processes are likely to depend more extensively on the creation and manipulation of situations and on symbiosis than on the internalization and enforcement of norms and values.

[44]Much of the following account of McCall's version of symbolic interactionism is drawn from George J. McCall and J. S. Simmons, *Identities and Interactions,* rev. (New York: The Free Press, 1978). Since that is a co-authored work, it may seem a slighting of his co-author to speak of McCall's version of symbolic interactionism. Given the context of other writings by the two, the attribution that has been made is reasonable. That is, many of McCall's other writings focus on the framework of symbolic interaction; among them are the following which enter secondarily into the present account: "Social Roles and Interaction," *Society Today* (Del Mar, Calif.: CRM Books, 1971):118–129; "The Social Looking Glass: A Sociological Perspective of Self-Development," in Theodore Mischel, ed., *The Self: Psychological and Philosophical Issues,* (Oxford: Blackwell, 1977), pp. 274–287; "A Symbolic Interactionist Approach to Attraction," in Ted L. Huston, ed., *Foundations of Interpersonal Attraction* (New York: Academic Press, 1974), pp. 217–231; "The Self: Conceptual Requirements from an Interactionist Perspective," unpublished paper presented at the 1977 annual meeting of the Section on Social Psychology, American Sociological Association, Chicago, September 5, 1977.

[45]McCall and Simmons, op. cit., p. ix.

a more adequate treatment of the impact of social structure on self and interaction, and towards a more conventional methodology. McCall begins with Kuhn but moves to a more complex and differentiated vision of the self that incorporates much more of Mead's "I" and is less bound by expectations of others tied to organizational roles. He also shifts to a more fluid phenomenological as well as constructed sense of social structure, an emphasis on the unique and idiosyncratic, and a less rigid methodological stance.

The heart of McCall's version is what is called the role-identity model. Before outlining that model, it is useful to suggest the nature of the assumptions and preliminary conceptualizations that underpin it.

> In the first place, man is a mammal, of quite ordinary properties, and is subject to all the blind determinisms of his anatomy, chemistry, and physiology.... Yet, at the same time, man lives in a symbolic universe not unlike Plato's realm of ideals....[46]

Thus, the beginning point for McCall is an imagery of man's nature, predicament, and fate that sees man as living a double existence in two very different worlds. He lives in a world of ideals; but he constantly does things based on forces other than conscious, reasoned choice premised on ideal considerations. Man does things, of which he is only partially aware, for reasons that are obscure to him. He is a brooding, introspective animal who lives in a social world and so must legitimate his actions not only to himself but to others. To maintain a shaky hold on ideals, man becomes a rhetorician: he seeks to persuade others as well as himself that things are as he construes them. Thus reality is something that is debated, compromised, and legislated.

The foregoing is a somewhat poetic way of asserting that man is a symbol-using animal, and the world he lives in is a symbolic, constructed world. Symbols, language, and the role-taking ability implied by symbols and language, transform man's behavior into conduct, and conduct is the special subject matter of social psychology. Park is quoted approvingly on this score:

[46]Ibid., pp. 38-39.

Conduct is that form of behavior we expect in man when he is conscious of the comment that other men are making, or are likely to make upon his actions. . . .

In human society every act of every individual tends to become a gesture, since what one does is always an indication of what one intends to do. The consequence is that the individual in society lives a more or less public existence, in which all his acts are anticipated, checked, inhibited, or modified by the gestures and the intentions of his fellows. It is this social conflict, in which every individual lives more or less in the mind of every other individual, that human nature and the individual may acquire their most characteristic and human traits.[47]

The role-identity model is a theory of conduct formulated in terms of the kind of social conflict described in Park's statement. The model builds upon a set of key concepts: interaction; social act and social object; the self; and the dramaturgical perspective.

The concept of interaction implies a pattern of reciprocal influence or interdependence between two elements: a deterministic relationship between two events that must be treated as a *joint* function, as a mutual or reciprocal influence. It is interaction which is the object of the theorizing contained in the role-identity model.

The concepts of social act and social object are taken from Mead. In Mead's view, acts are *released* by configurations of stimuli that an animal *seeks out* in order to fulfill impulses. The animal acts on its world and creates the objects in its environment. Involved here is the distinction between "things," bundles of stimuli that exist independently of the animal, and "objects" which come into existence in the course of an act. The same "thing" can be many objects: a tomato may be food in the context of one act, and an expression of anger (when thrown at someone) in the context of another act. Social objects are the creations of social acts which involve coordinated activity of more than one actor: "stealing a base" is a social object created by the coordinated activity of a number of persons playing baseball.

---

[47]Robert E. Park, "Human Nature, Attitudes, and Mores," in Kimball Young, ed., *Social Attitudes* (New York: Holt, 1931), p. 36.

Also taken from Mead is the concept of "self." McCall treats the self in terms of Mead's metaphorical "inner forum," the internalized conversation of the "I" and the "me," in which continuous self-appraisal is carried on using standards internalized from significant others and elaborated by the person himself. Added to the self, however, is a third component, character, a notion arising out of the dramaturgical perspective which suggests thinking of the self as composed of an actor or performer (the "I") and an internal audience (the "me"). It also suggests a view of self as character, a person with a distinctive organization of statuses, motives, traits, habits, and mannerisms.

These assumptions and concepts are used in the formulation of a set of basic principles underlying symbolic interaction.[48] These principles are:

1. Man is a planning animal, constructing plans out of bits and pieces supplied by culture.
2. Things take on meaning in relation to plans; the meaning of a thing is its implications for plans of action being constructed, so a thing may have different meanings relative to different plans.
3. We act toward things in terms of their meanings; a plan of action is executed, contingent on the meaning for that plan of things encountered.
4. Consequently, every thing encountered must be identified and its meaning discovered.
5. For social plans of action, meaning must be consensual; if meanings are not clear, they are hammered out through the rhetoric of interaction resulting in the creation of social objects.
6. The basic thing to be identified in any situation are the persons themselves; identities of actors in a situation must be consensually established.
7. Identity, meaning, and social acts are the stuff of drama; as drama involves parts to be played, roles implicit in the parts must be conceived and performed in ways expressive of the role. The construc-

[48]It is important to recognize that McCall regards symbolic interaction as only one of many interactive processes, including exchange, task performance, social control, etc., simultaneously involved in concrete interaction. It is, however, a key process: ". . . in most instances these additional processes take place within the arena carved out by symbolic interaction." Ibid., p. 58.

tion of social conduct involves roles and characters, props and supporting casts, and scenes and audiences.

8. Identification of persons is most often in terms of roles and characters. We identify by placing things in systematically related categories of role systems, status systems, systems of social types, or contrastive sets of social categories.[49]

Emerging from these principles are a number of distinctive conceptual requirements with respect to the self. The self as process entails an individual intending (planning) to be a particular kind of person; and the kind of person the self is striving to be will most often derive from systems of roles, statuses, social types or social categories. The key means through which intentions are appraised and performance monitored is through anticipating the reactions of other persons to plans and performances. This appraisal and monitoring takes place through a psycholinguistic process, often in the form of internalized, multipart conversation. There is a phenomenal aspect of the self (the self as character performed) as well as an active aspect (the self as performer) and a reactive aspect (the self as audience).

Further, while the structure of the self involves cognitive and affective responses to the self, more pivotal than self-cognitions and self-feelings and are self-judgments in the sense of appraisal of intentions and self-intervention. That structure, too, given the multiplicity of situations and roles in which people find themselves, must be seen as involving multiple conceptions of self rather than a global or unitary view of self. These multiple conceptions are principally role-based conceptions; they are "role-identities," or views of oneself in the role. These are to be distinguished from conceptions of roles or of others in those roles, for there is considerable and inevitable idiosyncratic variation in role-identities, in part as a consequence of attempts to achieve a better fit among them as a unique set adapted to performer characteristics and to a particular set of audiences. The various role-identities that make up the self are not on par with one another; some will be more prominent, i.e.,

[49]George J. McCall, "The Self: Conceptual Requirements from an Interactionist Perspective," op. cit., pp. 5–8.

central or important to the individual. And there will be considerable situational variation in likelihood of occurrence, independent of prominence, since every successive situation calls for a renewed assessment and decision concerning one's identity.

The symbolic interactionist perspective requires that self as structure and self as process be conceptually integrated; this means viewing people as persons—as active, constructivist, problem-solving, intentional actors capable of recognizing and communicating with other persons. Symbolic interactionist theoretical accounts are developed on the pivotal principle that there are reciprocal effects between self and social interaction.

The foregoing paragraphs suggest the central elements of the role-identity model. Some expansion of the skeletal sketch, however, will provide a better feel for McCall's version of symbolic interactionism.

A key to symbolic interactionism is the identification of persons and other things; without establishing the meanings of persons and other things, social acts could not occur. Identification of persons involves giving them a social identity by placing them in categories referring to unique individuals. Personal identities are the pegs upon which social identities and biography are hung; social identities are required if the individual is to be recognized from one occasion to another as the same person, and this is a requisite of the construction of stable social relationships.

Identifying persons in terms of social positions affords lead time in coping with them; such identification enables a preliminary specification of the relevance of others to plans of action, and may have implications for modification of conduct. However, expectations held for a given position will not serve as a genuine guide to action for they are too vague and incomplete to do so. The interactive role, or actual role performance, is improvised not only to take into account the demands of a position but also to reflect one's character and self-conception. Positional demands are modified to blend with these; role performance is expressive of the particular personality that happens to occupy the given position and represents the way the person comes to grips with the general expectations held toward someone in his or her position.

These considerations lead to the central concept of role-identity: the character and the role that an individual devises as an occupant of a particular social position. Less formally, it is one's imaginative view of being and acting as an occupant of a position.[50] As this suggests, a role-identity is usually idealized; the imaginations of the self involved often have the character of vicarious performances involving specific known others. Thus, real others are built into the content of a role-identity. One consequence is that role-identities change as persons and institutions flow into and out of the person's life.

Role-identities exert their influence on everyday life. They are a primary source of plans; they provide the criteria for appraising one's actual performances; they give meaning to a daily routine by largely determining interpretations of situations, events, and others encountered. They go far towards determining the objects in one's world, particularly self and others.

Conventional expectations—social roles—provide the structural framework for role-identities; personal elaborations are variations on culturally established themes. Each identity has two aspects, the conventional and the idiosyncratic, with relative proportion of these varying among persons and among identities of the same person. But as idealized and partially idiosyncratic conceptions of oneself, role-identities are often jarred and embarrassed by the realities of life; and persons are faced with the problem of devising perspectives that allow them to maintain their views of self, to legitimate their role-identities.

Legitimation is accomplished primarily via role-performances. Identities are not only for one's own consumption; others demand that a person claim some identity for they need cues to classify others as well. Others need to be persuaded of a person's claims; otherwise they will not accept the claims and their demands that a person be identifiable will not be met. The actor requires role-support: reactions and performances by others, the implications of which confirm one's imaginative view of oneself as an occupant of a position. That role-support is given primarily in response to role-performances.

[50]McCall and Simmons, op. cit., p. 65.

Identities are in continual need of legitimation, from others and from oneself: ". . . all things being equal, each of us is his own most important audience, for, unlike other audiences, this one cannot be escaped."[51] Role-performances are never perfect, role-support never total; there is always some tension between the reality of one's identity and discrepant impressions from the external world. One distinctive motive of human beings is the compelling and perpetual drive to acquire support for idealized conceptions of self. To do so, they seek interactions and audiences to obtain support from others and as opportunities for enactments through which they can give the self role-support through enriched, internal perspectives. Human beings seek to live their lives in the light of their role-identities. If they fail to do so, if they are not "legitimate" in their own eyes or the eyes of others, they will still seek to foster the social impression that they are legitimate through acquiring role-support.

The picture is complicated by the fact that everyone has many role-identities woven into a complex pattern. They mutually influence one another and are organized into a more or less systematically related (but not necessarily integrated or cohesive) whole. A major feature of this organization of role-identities is a loosely patterned hierarchy of prominence, or relative importance. Prominence is a function of those identities we come closest to living up to in our own view of things, and of those views of self which have been (and to what degree) supported by others. More important to prominence, however, is the degree to which the individual has committed him- or herself to the particular role-identity: has staked self-esteem on it, has invested resources in it, and has received both extrinsic and intrinsic gratifications from it. How these factors are weighed varies from person to person.

Some of these sources of prominence come from oneself, some from the audiences before which a performance is staged. Since members of those audiences are also performers in an encounter, there develop exchange relationships in which social support of identities and of intrinsic and extrinsic gratification is the coin.

[51]Ibid., p. 71.

Various role-identities give rise to many concrete performances, and a given role-identity suggests a number of alternative lines of action. Not all possibilities are compatible. What content ought to be chosen to maximize possible profits? Prominence provides a partial solution by contributing to a salience hierarchy,[52] an ordering of role-identities as possible performances in a situation. The salience hierarchy represents a situational self, not the ideal self represented by the prominence hierarchy.

Apart from prominence, the salience of role-identities is affected by the degree to which an identity is in need of support or legitimation; by the person's need or desire for the kinds and amounts of intrinsic and extrinsic gratifications to be gained through a performance in terms of a role-identity; and by the perceived opportunity for the profitable enactment of the role-identity under the circumstances at hand. An actual performance of any person involves a number of role-identities; and the subset the person tries to build into a performance constitutes the character he seeks to assume in that encounter. The person will improvise an interactive role expressive of a self-structure or character. But character and role cannot be chosen only on the basis of a salience hierarchy; choice is substantially influenced by the audience of a performance. Thus character and role are social objects jointly determined in the interaction of performer and audience.

The salience of role-identities, the situational self, is in turn affected by the rewards received in interaction. All of the determinants of salience, except prominence, are immediately affected; in general, the greater the discrepancy between rewards and desires, the greater the positive impact on salience. The correspondence between one's own expectations regarding a performance and the rewards obtained, also affects the salience of role-identities; what is important here is not so much the direct effect of others' expectations but one's own expectations. Others' evaluation

[52]Ibid., p. 82. This conception of identity salience is not that presented in Chapter 3, which more closely corresponds to McCall's use of prominence. At some point, such terminological confusions will disappear, as common ideas receive common labels. For the time being, however, representing the variants of symbolic interactionism reasonably argues for maintaining the language as it appears in the literature.

may be built into one's own self-expectations, and self-expectations are an average of sorts of social expectations, but the latter always filter through the former.

Self-expectations, like the identities to which they relate, are subject to change over time in content and relative importance. They are an intrinsic component of role-identities, a major link between the individual and his environment, for they are the empirical gambles on which the individual stakes his self-conceptions. More closely specified than social expectations, they are standards persons apply to their actions. And, given the nature of identities as idealized conceptions of self, their application means that persons wil generally judge themselves as falling short.

This discrepancy between performance and idealized images, between role-identity and the social support received, again poses the problem of legitimation. A number of mechanisms to "make things right" are available. They include building short-term credit with self and others that sustains "poor" performances, selective perception of cues, selective interpretation of audiences' responses, withdrawing from the field, switching to a role-identity likely to be more successful, rationalization, scapegoating, disavowal of the performer's claim to the identity, and rejection or deprecation of any audience withholding role-support.

Sometimes such mechanisms fail and the person cannot escape the awareness that an important audience has judged him a failure in a serious role-performance. Then, the attempt can be made to alter the salience of role-identities. We learn to adapt to such painful experience by hedging bets, by being more cautious in commitments, and by adopting an interactional strategy of minimizing losses rather than maximizing gains. Such strategies, ironically, mean that success in realizing ideal images in interaction is less achievable.

If all mechanisms fail, the individual may feel a generalized sense of self-derogation and unworthiness, and may even move toward self-destruction. These possibilities, however, are mitigated by overevaluation of performance by self and by others close to the person. "In-groups" function to provide mutual maintenance and reinforcement of members' self-conceptions. More generally, persons learn

to perceive and arrange encounters in which safe enactment of the characters they want to be is possible; and they
learn to avoid those situations, acts, and persons that
threaten role-identities.

More might be said about the role-identity model, but the
foregoing represents its major features. It is obvious that in
many ways there are parallels to, and some departures
from, the alternative versions of symbolic interactionism
already presented. Some comment on these will be reserved
for the next chapter.

We move now to the work of two scholars who have not
yet developed complete statements, but whose work is relevant to this review of symbolic interactionism. They are
Eugene A. Weinstein[53] and Peter J. Burke.

Eugene Weinstein

An effort to develop an integrated framework for the analysis of social interaction that preserves the special strengths
of symbolic interactionism, exchange, and structural-functionalism, yet does no violence to the essential tenets of
any,[54] is Weinstein's vehicle for comments on symbolic interactionism. Noting the debate that emerged from a
change in the focus of sociology from process to structure,
he also notes that symbolic interactionists are the inheri-
tors of the argument that society is social process and that
they remain "persistent evangelists" for the view of society
as an unending stream of interaction process.

Weinstein shares this view, and suggests that the real

[53]Once again we are faced with a jointly-authored work which contains the
core of what is being attributed to one of the two authors. Again, the reading is
justified by the fuller context of writings from the authors. The work in question
is Eugene A. Weinstein and Judith M. Tanur, "Meanings, Purposes, and Structural
Resources in Social Interaction," *The Cornell Journal of Social Relations,* 11
(Spring 1976):105–110. Other of Weinstein's relevant writings include: "The Self
and Social Structure from a Symbolic Interactionist Perspective," unpublished
paper presented to the Section on Social Psychology, American Sociological Association, Chicago, September 5, 1977; "Role and Interpersonal Style as Components
of Social Interaction," *Social Forces,* 45 (December, 1966):210–216 (with Mary
Glenn Wiley and William DeVaughn); "The Development of Interpersonal Com-
petence," in David Goslin, ed., *Handbook of Socialization Theory and Research,*
(New York: Russell Sage Foundation, 1969); "Tasks, Bargains and Identities in
Social Interaction," *Social Forces,* 42 (May, 1964):451–456 (with Paul Deutschberger); "Some Dimensions of Altercasting," *Sociometry,* 26 (December,
1963):454–466 (with Paul Deutschberger).

[54]Weinstein and Tanur, op. cit.

strength of symbolic interactionism is its sensitivity to the emergent properties of interaction. The episode of interaction is a temporary world in itself for the participants, and in such worlds social structure finds its concrete expression.

Out of an overemphasis of this strength comes certain "excesses" of one wing of symbolic interactionism, excesses not shared by all versions. Seeing social processes as the interplay of minded individuals leads to one excess: an injunction against quantitative methods as a matter of faith rather than style. Weinstein argues that recognizing the qualitative contents of consciousness does not mean that the exterior expression of these contents cannot be coded, classified, and counted just as the person codes, classifies, and counts in dealing with the richness of his own life; and he argues that no one can attend to the richness of all experience, that categoric systems for collapsing and coding information is what makes mind possible in the first place, and that informal counting of occurrences is what we mean by experience. Observing that any research involves a trade-off between qualitative but vague richness dependent upon the perceptive skills of the individual analyst and the more precise, replicable, narrow identification of patterns, he suggests that some symbolic interactionists beg the question of this trade-off in their rejection of quantitative analyses. In practice, this is seen as leading to the proliferation of sensitizing concepts used for describing the content of people's consciousness; work at its best sensitive and compelling, but at its worst obscuring the essential distinction between definition and explanation and being trapped in taxonomic formalism.

Weinstein believes that a sensitizing orientation can lead to work that is prospective, quantitative, and oriented to explanation rather than being only retrospective, qualitative, and oriented to understanding. Recasting the insights gained from a phenomenological stance into a measurement framework can make it possible to assess the degree of consensus in intersubjectivity and reduce the reliance on perceptions of a single analyst. And the results of phenomenologically premised research can be incorporated into quantitative modes of analysis. Recognizing that there are always unlocatable limits to the extent of intersubjectivity, the problems in assuming isomorphism between the communicative intent of an actor and an analyst's reading of that intent, and the danger that an analyst's theoretical scheme will interfere with attempts to capture the meanings of those whose interactions the analyst is studying, the argument is not that quantification enables special insight, but that we ought not rule out techniques that can add power and sensitivity to individual judgment when the attempt is made to describe patterning in a set of observations.

A second excess follows from the almost exclusive concentration on events within an episode of interaction and on the people in it: neglect of the connectedness of episodes. Aggregated outcomes of many prior episodes of interaction link episodes. Participants in any episode of interaction must work within a framework provided by the prior interactions between others: informal understandings, codified rules, shared meanings, and material resources. To examine aggregated properties of episodes as a social system is legitimate, and one is not reifying aggregate properties to see them as contributing to the resources available to participants in a concrete episode of interaction. One can do so without denying that it is in the episode that resources become manifest, or that they are mediated through the consciousness of participants. And it is not necessary to reduce social structure to individual consciousness. Social-structural concepts are necessary to deal with the density and complexity of relations through which episodes are connected.

As Weinstein notes, structural-functional analyses start with this aggregate level. Within this frameqork, the concepts of status and role link structure and process. People are attached to structure in everyday interaction through normatively scripted roles. These role expectations are equipment individuals possess for participation in the social process. Internalized by individuals, they operate as self-regulatory mechanisms, becoming manifest in interaction with other individuals possessing complementary equipment. Weinstein argues that the burden carried by the concept of role in structural-functional analysis is too great, but that it is possible to modify it by including processual and contextual components. To do so, the symbolic interactionist concept of situational identity—the locus of all attributes and characterisitcs imputed to a person by those present in a given encounter—is introduced. Situational identities may include social positions, but are not limited to these; and, while positions may serve as bases for expectations and actions, they may set only broad limits for behavior, too broad to be of much import in determining which behavior will take place toward what end.

One cannot, in short, assume a fit between structural imagery and concrete social process. The degree to which a social encounter exhibits "roleness" is problematic and open to investigation. Norms and roles are part of but not all of the meanings accessible to participants in interaction, and they can be used as resources in interaction. "The extent, the conditions and the means by which such structural resources are brought into play, are thus investigated within a context of discovery rather than serving as the analyst's arbitrarily imposed metaphor."[55]

Exchange theory sees people as packages of hierarchical interests, outcome values, or preferences. But discussions of such are atomistic; there is little concern for how values or outcomes are interrelated within the individual, though they probably are. Again, a symbolic interactionist concept is introduced: the self-system; and the claim is that the self provides a useful way of viewing the integration of values or outcomes. The overt manifestation in interaction of the self is the individual's situational identity; these can be the loci of rewards and costs. A person's principal motivation in an exchange relationship may be to receive affirmation from another of a desired or required identity. Or establishing a particular identity may be a requisite for other purposes: to be defined as essential to the group will give a person leverage in dealing with it. In either case, exchanges involve negotiations and renegotiations about who is "really" who in the situation.

Social structure, in the terms used above, consists of the aggregated outcomes of episodes of interaction and their linkages. How are the links forged? In a speculative response that translates across structural, processual, and cognitive levels of analysis—and to reduce the former two to their cognitive roots—Weinstein offers the concept of

[55]Ibid., p. 107.

"trace."[56] His discussion of this concept and its implications contains interesting potentials for the future development of symbolic interactionism.

As Weinstein notes, the symbolic interactionist emphasis on process leads to a view of social structure as something that happens rather than something that is: social structure is a continuous accomplishment through the coordination of action made possible through symbolic mediation. Social structure is the patterning of social process and becomes manifest in social process; yet, paradoxically, social process is episodic in that people come together and leave, begin and end social occasions. Traces link these episodes, thus traces are central to social structure.

Traces are residuals of experience available for retrieval as people organize their action by relating present experience to past experience in order to realize envisaged futures. They evoke purposes and suggest actions for accomplishing them; they may be internal or external. Imprints—images of the past that can be retrieved from short term memory and scanned—and templates—models or schematics of prior experience to be associated with a current stimulus event—are two major types of internal traces. Templates act as patterns for retrieval from long term storage, and they organize short term processing. Objects are one kind of external trace of past activity; objects are "triggered" by recognition of any aspect of an earlier stimulus configuration in which an object was experienced. Signs, a second form of external trace, are stimulus configurations that "trigger" templates. Both objects and signs can trigger templates, but signs are only related through convention to the templates they trigger. Some templates relate only to other templates and have no direct link to experience.

Returning to the linkages of episodes, and the function of traces in providing linkages, Weinstein notes that part of the work of any social encounter is to produce traces that will link the encounter to future encounters—explicitly through schedules and agendas, implicitly through a vast variety of less formal means. Traces also provide cues as to how an occasion is to be "framed," or defined, setting

---

[56]"The Self and Social Structure from a Symbolic Interactionist Perspective," op. cit.

boundary conditions and serving as resources for negotiation in the defining process. Planning encounters occur to generate traces, and to coordinate action and subsequent encounters. Implied here is a need to reorient thinking with respect to social structure. Sociological thinking emphasizes relationships between persons or institutional actors; the starting point for accounts of coordinated activity will also be understood in terms of the occasions of its occurrences and the linkages among these provided by traces.

A major concern of symbolic interactionism is the self-social structure relationship. The self, according to Weinstein, can stand in several relations to the organization of experience. At the most primitive level, the self is not implicated at all; there is no sense of self as reactive responder. At a second level, simple self-awareness exists; imprints contain the relation of self to the experience that it has undergone, and this permits complexity in organizing current experience. With language, a higher level is achieved; arbitrary symbols as signs for templates extend the reflexivity of the self, enabling not only self-awareness but self-interaction. The product of that interaction is situated activity. Weinstein speculates that the self acts as a master template, importantly implicated in generating envisaged futures; and from this point of view the self is a set of purposes. The self generates purposes through the organization of current experiences and it mobilizes expressive resources for pursuing those purposes. It also has a reflexive function as a template to connect these two functions. And it is linked through traces to social structure in two ways: (1) traces, as elements of culture, indicate the requirements of occasions, defining who one can (or cannot) be and still achieve the practical end of the coordinated activity; and (2) traces provide resources for realizing identities in ongoing interaction.

Peter J. Burke

Burke's work in a symbolic interactionist vein begins with the observation that while the constructs of self, self-concept, and identity are quite widely used in social psychology and sociology, their use in empirical research has been quite limited; and with the assertion that for research to catch up with theoretical development, a technique to measure identities in a satisfactory manner is required.[57] This is not to say, however, that Burke's work is of only narrow methodological interest. He takes the position, often asserted but more frequently ignored than honored, that the process of measurement must be based on a theoretical understanding of the phenomenon to be measured.[58] Consequently, he considers the theoretical properties of the concept of role/identity and in so doing contributes much of conceptual and theoretical interest to symbolic interactionism more generally.

The term role/identity is taken from McCall and Simmons. Role/identities are subunits of a multifaceted self. The term intends to stress the tie between components of the self and locations in the social structure, which is emphasized by McCall and Simmons, by Stryker, and by others.[59] It is this tie between components of the self and social structure that Burke terms a most important development of self theory and credits with making more tractable the problematics of the link between identity and performance.[60]

Developments in ideas about role/identities have produced a number of common conceptions: identities are meanings attributed by the person to the self as an object in a social situation or social role; identities are relational; identities are reflexive; identities operate indirectly; and identities are a source of motivation. Each of these conceptual properties of role/identities has measurement consequences.

It is Osgood's[61] "representational mediation process" that supplies the meaning of "meaning" in the initial conceptual property. Self-meanings come to be known by the per-

[57]Peter J. Burke and Judy C. Tully, "The Measurement of Role/Identity," *Social Forces,* 55 (June, 1977):881–897.

[58]Peter J. Burke, "The Self: Measurement Requirements from an Interactionist Perspective," unpublished revised version of a paper presented to the Section on Social Psychology, American Sociological Association, Chicago, September 5, 1977.

[59]George J. McCall and J. T. Simmons, op. cit.; Stryker, "Identity Salience and Role Performance," op. cit.

[60]Peter J. Burke, "The Self: Measurement Requirements from an Interactionist Perspective," op. cit., p. 1.

[61]C. C. Osgood, G. J. Suci, and P. H. Tannenbaum, *The Measurement of Meaning* (Urbana: University of Illinois Press, 1957).

son through interaction with others in situations. Others respond as if the person had an identity appropriate to a role performance; it is through such responses that the meanings of the self are learned. These responses are cues to appropriate role performances; and they imply an identity appropriate to that role performance. As Mead understood, one's acts develop meaning through reactions of others and invoke in the person the responses that are invoked in others. This conceptualization calls for a measurement procedure that captures the multiple underlying dimensions of meaning that comprise the self. These dimensions can be conceptualized as a multidimensional semantic space, and measurement involves mapping the space and locating persons' role/identities—their individual self-meanings—within that space.

Identities are relational in the sense that they are related to roles. They are relational as well in two other senses. Identities are related to other identities; just as roles are defined by their relation to counterroles, so identity as an internal component of a role is defined in relation to counteridentities. Identities also relate to one another through being organized into a salience hierarchy.[62] Since high-ranking identities are more likely to be invoked in situations rather than lower-ranking, and to be invoked along with those of lower ranking, identities at the top of the salience hierarchy are used to organize and to order those that are lower. Implied for measurement purposes is that identities cannot be measured in isolation from other identities; they necessarily must be measured in terms of commonalities among persons similarly situated and in terms of differences with persons in counterpositions. Too, the idea of a salience hierarchy implies that the measurement of high ranking identities will be less problematic than the measurement of low-ranking identities, since by definition they are more likely to be invoked in different situations and since, as organizers of low-ranking identities, they will be relatively stable through time.

Symbolic interactionists, following Mead and James, have always emphasized the reflexive character of self.

[62]See the discussion of this concept in Chapter 3, and see the discussion of the related concept of a prominence hierarchy in the review of McCall's work in this chapter.

Burke suggests that the import of reflexivity lies in its consequences. Reflexivity is the feedback to the self of the consequences of the processes that are the self: identities influence performances and performances are assessed by the self for their identity implications. What feedback shows about an identity is compared with that identity in terms of the same categories of meaning that define the identity in the initial instance. This argues that the feedback can be controlled by changing performances until there is some degree of correspondence between the perceived self and the "real" self. In measurement terms, what is thus called for is an assessment of the strength of the corrective responses when a performance is "off target," and an assessment of what it is that the person corrects.

The conceptualization of identities as operating indirectly is addressed to the issue of self as process or structure, the idea of self as undergoing constant change versus the idea of self as having temporal stability. Burke proposes that an identity influences a role performance through the construction of a self-image and that it is the self-image that directly influences performance. The image is conceived of as a "current working copy" of the identity. As working copy, it is subject to continual revision, editing, and updating in response to situational variations and demands. Identities change, but not as rapidly as images. They are a kind of idealized picture of the self-in-role which motivates performance but whose realization depends on contingencies and exigencies of the situation of interaction. The image, not the identity, guides the immediate interaction. The identity guides the construction and maintenance of the image; and the image influences the identity, although this impact is likely to be small relative to the reverse. Thus the image acts as a buffer between the identity and the vicissitudes of normal interaction.

Burke notes that competent performance in an interactive situation requires a mental model of the situation and of the roles and relationships of the performers in the situation. Role/identities are not good working models precisely because they are relatively stable and removed from the demands of the situation. The image, constructed in the situation, is the working model for constructing interaction; it is flexible enough to accommodate role-taking as well as role-making, role enactment as well as role construction. Burke adds to this picture an important complication: one's performance feeds back directly on image and allows keeping performance consistent with the image; but one's performance has as well important implications for the self-images of other interactants, which images influence their performances and which performances in turn have an impact on one's image.

The final conceptual property of role/identities reviewed by Burke is that they are sources of motivation.[63] Identities motivate through defining behavior: the classification of social objects including the self and others invokes shared expectations for behavior; i.e., meanings have action implications. Burke offers a series of refinements of this idea. If identities as meanings are located in semantic space, and have action implications, then identities that are close to one another in that semantic space ought have a very similar action implications. Further, the acts and performances that have identity implications are also classified and located in that same semantic space. As earlier suggested, the relation between the identity and performance is monitored for its implications with respect to that identity. Thus, the distance in semantic space between the meanings of identity and performance is, in effect, measured in evaluating one's own and others' performances. Ideally, the observer or analyst will use a measurement procedure which accomplishes analogous results: the location of identities and behaviors in n-dimensional space. Finally, the underlying dimensions of the semantic space used to locate identities and behaviors are defined by cultural standards. Only if this is so can there be the shared standards for assessing and identifying the individuals and behaviors that meaningful social interaction requires.

Burke summarizes the foregoing conceptual and theoretical discussion by raising a set of questions to be asked in assessing measures of role/identity:

1. Does the measure locate the identity in a semantic space defined by shared cultural standards concerning the *dimensions* of that space and the *locations* of typical-,

---

[63]For an early and influential attempt to see identities as motivational forces, see Nelson N. Foote, "Identification as the Basis for a Theory of Motivation," *American Sociological Review,* 16 (February, 1951):14–21.

     stereotypical-, ideal- or normatively defined identities *within that space*?

2. Does the measure recognize and incorporate the link that exists between the internal identity and the external role?

3. Does the measure recognize and incorporate the relationship between identities and counter-identities—that people define themselves as much by what they are not as by what they are?

4. Does the measure incorporate the reflexive nature of the self in some sort of corrective procedure to increase reliability and indicate further characteristics of the individual's image space?

5. Does the measure recognize the indirectness of the link between identity and performance (which exists both in social situations generally as well as in the measurement situation more specifically)?

6. Does the procedure recognize the probabilistic nature of the image which intervenes between identity and performance?[64]

There is little utility, for present purposes, in a presentation of the measurement procedures Burke has or is developing that reflect the requisites discussed above.[65] The discussion can end by simply noting Burke's view that if empirical research is to catch up with theoretical developments in symbolic interactionism, techniques used—apart from the desiderata already stated—must result in a quantitative measure that can be used in multivariate data analysis. This requirement reflects Burke's belief that not only is the self complex, the real world is as well.

A Concluding Note

This chapter has reviewed variants of symbolic interactionism. It cannot be said that those reviewed, along with the version presented in Chapter 3, cover the spectrum fairly. Instead, and with the singular exception of Blumer's symbolic interactionism, the concentration has been on the

---

[64]Op. cit., pp. 10–11.

[65]Suffice it to say that the procedures currently in use involve semantic differential descriptions and discriminant function analysis, with coefficients provided by the latter used to locate role-identities via application to individuals' own descriptions of self-in-role.

work of scholars who are oriented toward the development of an empirically based, testable set of general theoretical propositions, who take seriously—on theoretical, conceptual, and empirical levels—the realities of social structure, and who do not rule out in principle any of the scientific methods and techniques available for the study of human behavior.

Even within these limits, however, the versions covered cannot be said to be carbon copies of one another. True, there is common acceptance of some very general principles; and, beyond this, there seems to be an emergent consensus on important matters of concept, theory, and procedure. But there is difference and disagreement as well. There are differences in just how "determinative" social structure is seen, and in what ways, with respect to self and interactional processes. There are differences in just how social structure in conceptualized; differences in just what range of social and personal behavior symbolic interactionism is taken to be responsible for and to; differences in analytic and theory-building strategies; and so on.

Clearly, the various versions of symbolic interactionism are all primarily on the level of theoretical or conceptual frameworks and not of theory, although there are differences in the degree to which one or another moves in the direction of theory. And just as clearly, every version is open to critical comment, although not necessarily in the same degree to the same critical comment. The final chapter turns to the business of criticisms of symbolic interactionism that have been and can be made.

5

Appraisals

Introduction

The point has been iterated frequently in the preceding pages, but it is worth repeating yet again as a preface to this chapter: there is no single symbolic interactionism. Thus, while it may be that all of the versions reviewed are, in fact, subject to some particular criticism, it is also true that a criticism applicable to one version may have little or no application to another. Clearly, for example, the methodological criticisms that Blumer directs at sociology in general are appropriate to the version of symbolic interactionism of Chapter 3 and (in perhaps varying degree) to all versions except that of Blumer presented in Chapter 4. (Whether one accepts these critical comments or what one makes of them is obviously another matter.) And, just as clearly, the negative commentary in prior chapters with respect to Blumer's lack of a "proper" appreciation of social structure does not apply (again, in varying degree and whatever one makes of the commentary) to the alternatives to his particular vision of symbolic interactionism.

It is important to consistently keep in mind the possibility that the virtues of one version of symbolic interactionism are the vices of others. This is especially true because many appraisals, whether critical or appreciative, do not appear to be aware of the internal variations that exist within this framework. In particular, the assumption is often made

136

that the work of Blumer and the content of symbolic interactionism are largely isomorphic. While—given Blumer's invention of the term—there is some historical justification for this assumption, the term has taken on meaning beyond that provided by its inventor. One might argue the appropriateness of this expanded meaning, but it is clear that this volume has dealt with symbolic interactionism in its broader sense.

In some respect or another, the versions of symbolic interactionism in Chapter 3 and (with the exception of Blumer's) Chapter 4 have incorporated elements of role theory. Since that is the case, it seems wise to include in this appraisal some attention to role theory, albeit in a limited way. We begin with this task, and then move to a somewhat more thorough look at the imputed problems of the variety of symbolic interactionisms.

A Limited Appraisal of Role Theory

Since the scope of this work has not been extended to a full review of role theory itself, but only to aspects of it as incorporated into one or another version of the symbolic interactionist framework, our critical attention is attenuated. Ralph Turner's theoretical work, as noted, began with a critique of role theory, and that critique is discussed in Chapter 4. Also in Chapter 4, what Blumer has had to say, both conceptually and methodologically, is in effect a critique of role theory as it developed in the writings of Linton, Parsons, Merton, and others. Neither Turner's nor Blumer's appraisals of role theory will be repeated here; rather, the commentary of Dennis H. Wrong and Aaron V. Cicourel serves as the basis of the remarks that follow.

Wrong[1] argues that contemporary American sociology holds an oversocialized conception of humans and an over-integrated conception of society. Posing the "Hobbesian question"—how is social order possible?—he suggests that sociological theory as formulated and influenced by Talcott Parsons provides two main answers, each of which serves to deny the meaningfulness of the original question. One

---

[1]Dennis H. Wrong, "The Oversocialized Conception of Man in Modern Sociology," *American Sociological Review,* 26 (April, 1961):184-193.

answer asserts that the prime motivation of a human is the desire to achieve a positive self-image through meeting the expectations of others. Wrong claims that the stress on the concept of "role" as crucially linking person and social structure, serves to direct attention to the immediate situation of social interaction. While valuable in enabling a better grasp of the complexity of a highly differentiated social structure, this focus leads to an image of the human as a roleplayer, eagerly or anxiously responding to expectations of other role players in multiple group settings. Reified as socialized man, the status-seeker of contemporary sociology, this image has its purposes so long as it is not taken as the "whole truth."

Among the deficiencies of such an image, according to Wrong, is its neglect of "moral man": the human as guided by a built-in superego, or internalized norms. The internalization of norms, interpreted as both affirmation of and behavioral conformity to institutionalized norms and roles, is the second answer sociological theory gives to the Hobbesian question. But the power of this second response, to make up for the inadequacies of the first, is vitiated by the tendency to interpret internalization precisely as affirmation and behavioral conformity, thus failing to provide for inner conflict, for tensions between impulses and superego controls which make behavioral outcomes problematic, and for motivations that buck the system.

In Wrong's view, these answers do scant justice to the dialectic process in which conformity and rebellion, social norms and their violation, and instinctual humans and social order, work against and through one another. As he says:

That material interests, sexual drives, and the quest for power have often been over-estimated as human motives is no reason to deny their reality. To do so is to suppress one term of the dialectic ... as completely as the other term is suppressed by those who deny the reality of man's "normative orientation" or reduce it to the effect of coercion, rational calculation, or mechanical conditioning.[2]

Humans have both beast and angel in their nature, and these forces are resistant to socialization. Thus humans are

[2]Ibid., p. 191.

social, says Wrong, but not entirely socialized; their nature creates resistance to socialization in terms of the norms of any society. Such a view of human beings is a necessary corrective to the implicit view characterizing sociological theory stemming from an overstress on the stability and integration of society which leads to "imagining that man is the disembodied, conscience driven, status-seeking phantom of current theory."[3]

All of which is to say that the relation between norms and roles (as elemental features of social structure and behavior) is intrinsically problematic, and not to be resolved simply by invoking the conceptual apparatus of role theory. From quite a different starting point, these same criticisms of role theory as offering an overly structured and static image of the relation of society and social person appear in the work of Aaron V. Cicourel.[4]

It is Cicourel's intent to go beyond the sociological expression of faith in the assumed relationship of social process and social structure by providing an explicit foundation for integrating the two. As a step in accomplishing this intent, he offers a fundamental critique of the concepts of status, role, norm, and social interaction, i.e., of role theory. His argument is fundamentally that such concepts are of limited utility in specifying how the person negotiates everyday behavior. "It is not clear that terms like 'status' and 'role' are relevant categories for the actors nor relevant for the observer's understanding of the action scene he seeks to describe."[5]

Arguing the necessity of linking the actor's strategies of interaction with the social analyst's structural framework, Cicourel asserts that the structural framework of status and role seldom points to interactional consequences. That is,

[3]Ibid., p. 193. An alternative to this emphasis on " the beast and angel" in humans as a *necessary* corrective is one which comes directly out of role theory itself. A differentiated society leads directly to the notion that conflict, internal and otherwise, is endemic, and to the idea that resistance to the socialization impact of one group can be premised on allegiances to another *rather* than arising out of human biology.

[4]Particularly, for present purposes, *Cognitive Sociology* (New York: Free Press, 1972). There are many ethnomethodologies, as well as symbolic interactionisms, but since that variety cannot be dealt with, Cicourel is taken as illustrative of the ethnomethodological movement and its critique of role theoretic notions.

[5]Ibid., p. 13. The title of the essay being drawn on is "Interpretive Procedures and Normative Rules in the Negotiation of Status and Role."

while traditional conceptual analyses presuppose consensus on the content of statuses and roles, and take for granted that these are known and clear, the reality is that they are anything but nonproblematic. Instead, concrete situations of action involve a dialetic between what appears to be structurally or institutionally invariant and what depends on actors' perceptions and interpretations. Vague features of statuses, roles, and norms unfold and become concretized over the course of interaction and alter, distort, or maintain institutionalized features. Thus the use of the language of status and role presupposes an actor's cognitive procedures and a theory of social meaning (a theory of how actors assign meanings to objects and events). The use of the abstract theoretical concepts masks rather than illuminates the inductive or interpretive procedures through which the actor produces behavior that the analyst may label as role behavior.

Cicourel's argument goes beyond asserting the constructed character of interaction; and his comment on the "masking" impact of role-theoretic concepts is extended to apply to Turner's emphasis on role-making as well as to the more static and normatively structured process of role-playing. What all such theoretical efforts lack and what disables them is the absence of explicit statements about how actors recognize relevant stimuli in the context of interaction and orient themselves so that they can generate an organized response that will be recognized as relevant to other interactants. What is missing, in brief, are assertions about basic interpretive procedures which "enable the actor to sustain a *sense of social structure* over the course of changing social settings...."[6] Such interpretive procedures[7] and the sense of social order that they provide are fundamental in order that consensus or shared agreement exist or be constructed. Thus, a surface normative order and a deep interpretive order, or sense of social structure, are

---

[6]Ibid., p. 27, emphasis in original.

[7]Ibid., p.34, an example of an interpretive procedure, taken from Schutz, is the "reciprocity of perspectives," which consists of two parts: (1) the first part instructs participants in interaction to assume that their mutual experiences of the interaction would be the same even were they to exchange places; and (2) the second part instructs interactants to disregard personal differences in how they assign meaning to everyday activity so that they can for practical purposes attend in the same way to issues at hand.

always in interaction; it is "absurd" to speak of one without the other. Clearly, from Cicourel's perspective, sociological theories cannot qualify as sound theories, if they fail to incorporate interpretive processes into their structures.

Both Wrong's and Cicourel's criticisms of role theory were formulated in relation to role theory per se, and not in reaction to symbolic interactionisms that incorporate elements of the role theoretic perspective. One ought ask whether they apply to their initial target; one must ask whether they apply—or apply with the same force—to the latter. Since Blumer's symbolic interactionism rejects, on essentially the same grounds as does Cicourel, structural concepts, at least that version of symbolic interactionism is exempt from much of Cicourel's evaluation.[8] And, of course, that part of Wrong's critique which simply argues the problematic nature of the linkages between social structure and behavior also fails to apply to Blumer. Wrong's insistence that motives—other than self-esteem through meeting others' expectations—enter the human equation is not troublesome in the context of Blumer's ideas: the self is the theoretical vehicle through which alternative motivations can enter behavior. However, insofar as one takes seriously Wrong's invocation of Freud and the animal nature of man and the implied importance of the nonrational and the unconscious in human action, Blumer's apparent emphasis on the reflexivity inherent in all human interaction is a flaw. There is little hint in Blumer's writings that reflexivity is a matter of degree or, indeed, may even be absent from behavior; thus the image of man in those writings is of a totally self-conscious creature whose choices are organized through maximally reflective processes.

The remaining versions of symbolic interactionism are differentially tarred by these critical brushes. The version in Chapter 3 is closest to structural role theory, and it is, at least potentially, most subject to Wrong's and Cicourel's criticisms. The discussion will proceed without further specification of differential applicability.

The recognition that social-structural categories do not "automatically" translate into behavior, and the related

---

[8]If, however, explicit statements about interpretive procedures are a requisite of sound sociological theory, the absence of such makes Blumer's formulations deficient from Cicourel's perspective.

view that it is inappropriate to conceive of man as a neutral carrier of others' expectations, is reflected in the use made of Turner's notion of role-making. That notion conceptualizes interaction as an arena in which preliminary definitions of the situation—of self, of other, and of setting—are tentatively asserted and played out, modified and even discarded as the interaction proceeds. Behavior is seen as an emergent out of this process; and not as predetermined by the structural elements entering into the preliminary definitions. At the same time, the import of social structure is not denied: it does impact on who is and is not brought into interactive contact, what preliminary definitions they are likely to hold, what interactional resources are available, and so on. For Cicourel, the reality of social structure is basically in the interactants' heads; he returns essentially to a Cooley-esque extreme in which society is transmuted into the *personal idea* of society, social structure into the idea of social structure. There is then, a tendency to deny the independent, objective bases of the constraints on interaction that are the social structure. Insofar as this is a reasonable reading of Cicourel's critical comment, at least some symbolic interactionists would simply assert its unacceptability.

The over-structured implications of role theory are modified importantly by symbolic interactionism's theoretical use of the concept of self. That concept permits both a theoretically legitimated opposition to social expectations and the incorporation of "material interests, sexual drives and quest for power," which Wrong asks sociological theory to recognize along with other role-related motivations. In important degree, then, the "oversocialized conception of man" criticism that can be made of role theory does not apply to symbolic interactionism when given the importance of the concept of the self within that framework. It can be added that a multifaceted conception of self in terms of multiple identities reinforces this assertion. Recognition that the self is a variable, that there are varying degrees of reflexivity involved in the full range of human actions, goes at least part of the way towards recognizing that habit, unconscious processes, and even (possibly) blind instinct can be operative in interaction.

There is in some statements of role theory itself—and especially in the elements of role theory incorporated into Chapter 3—a source of conflict which Wrong underplays in his critique. Wrong relies on Freud and on biology to introduce conflict into the social scene through the opposition of the individual and a monolithic society. If, however, society is not viewed as an integrated whole but rather as a congeries of crosscutting substructures—if, in brief, role conflict, as a structural and social psychological possibility, is taken seriously—then differing and contradictory expectations become a normal feature of social life and conformity becomes, from a role-theoretic standpoint, much more problematic than Wrong believes it to be.

To what degree is there force to Cicourel's insistence that explicit statements with respect to interpretive procedures be incorporated into an adequate sociological theory? The answer must be conditional: it depends on one's willingness to accept the view of theory espoused in Chapter 1. If all theories are partial and selective in their emphases—if a theory cannot include all variables and relationships among variables germane to the explanation of some phenomena of interest—then Cicourel's insistence is less forceful than it would otherwise be. Surely, a "total" explanation of human behavior has to incorporate such interpretive procedures as may exist—particularly if, as Circourel believes, they are the "deep structure" which gives order to surface variation. But just as surely, they can be left out if the intellectual problems one wishes to solve, as in role theory, can be handled by beginning one's theorizing with the end products of the interpretive procedures. In brief, then, the answer to the initial question is: it depends on what a theory is about. Having said that, it must be added that the aim of Cicourel's theorizing is to account for the course of interaction itself, and not for either the structure of the social person or the structure of organized social relationships. Insofar as it is the former that is the object of explanation, Cicourel's criticism has point.

Thus far, critical attention has been focused on role theory. But it is symbolic interactionism, not role theory, that is of central concern here, and it is to criticisms of symbolic interactionism that we now turn.

Major Criticisms Of Symbolic Interactionism: Statement And Appraisal

For the moment, the discussion will proceed without distinguishing among the various symbolic interactionisms, but simply reviewing the major criticisms that have been levelled at the perspective. Because, however, most "outsiders" tend to identify symbolic interactionism with Blumer and most "insiders" probably do as well, the criticisms were mainly formulated with his position in mind.[9]

A large critical literature has developed with respect to symbolic interactionism. Very early, Mead found it necessary to comment critically on the solipsism as well as the utopianism inherent in Cooley's thought.[10] And Mead's own formulations have been subject to negative, as well as positive, evaluation, much of it focusing on the vagueness and the ambiguity of central ideas[11] and on the indeterminancy introduced into his theory through the concept of the "I."[12] Then, too, the Blumer-Kuhn "debate"—largely carried on by adherents of the respective Chicago and Iowa "schools" —essentially represents the critique of one version of symbolic interactionism from the standpoint of another, and vice versa.

In more recent years, a number of critiques and appraisals of symbolic interactionism have appeared. The most extensive of these, perhaps, is that provided by Meltzer, Petras, and Reynolds.[13] Distinguishing between in-house

[9]In comparatively recent times, considerable critical attention has been paid to Erving Goffman and to the dramaturgical framework that Goffman preeminently represents. No attempt was made to cover Goffman's work as a variant form of symbolic interactionism in this volume, on the grounds that it did not fit the selection criteria on the basis of which choice was made. Thus, attention will not be given to criticisms specific to that work, with an exception introduced later. Gonos argues that Goffman is not in fact properly regarded as a symbolic interactionist, although the conventional wisdom so views him. See George Gonos, " 'Situation' versus 'Frame': The 'Interactionist' and the 'Structuralist' Analyses of Everyday Life," *American Sociological Review,* 42 (December, 1977) pp. 854-867.

[10]George H. Mead, "Cooley's Contribution to American Social Thought," *American Journal of Sociology,* 35 (1930):693–706.

[11]See, for example, Manford H. Kuhn, "Major Trends in Symbolic Interaction Theory in the Past Twenty-five Years," op. cit.; Bernard N. Meltzer, *The Social Psychology of George* Herbert Mead (Kalamazoo, Mich.: Center for Sociological Research, Western Michigan University, 1959); Herbert Blumer, *Symbolic Interactionism,* op. cit.

[12]For example, William L. Kolb, "A Critical Evaluation of Mead's 'I' and 'Me' Concepts," *Social Forces,* 22 (March, 1944):291–296.

[13]Op. cit., Chapter 3.

(interactionist) and outside (noninteractionist) criticisms, these authors develop a compendium of criticisms from the writings of Meltzer, Brittain, Denzin, Kuhn, and Hall (the in-house critics), and of Block, Smith, Ropers, Kanter, Gouldner, Shaskolski, Huber, and Lichtman (the outsiders).[14] As this list of names suggests, the points of criticisms are diverse and the perspectives from which the criticisms are made are varied.

Ignoring any number of more or less subtle variations, the fundamental criticisms of symbolic interactionism reduce to five:[15]

1. Key concepts, especially the concept of the self, are confused and imprecise and therefore cannot provide the basis for sound theory development.

2. Relatedly, there are serious methodological problems in the position. Its concepts are difficult if not impossible to "operationalize," the position generates few testable propositions, and it rejects scientific explanation in favor of intuitive insight or understanding.[16]

3. In its emphasis on meaning and on the import of reflexive thought in behavior, it overlooks the perva-

[14]Bernard N. Meltzer, *The Social Psychology of George Herbert Mead,* op. cit., and "Mead's Social Psychology," in Jerome G. Manis and Bernard N. Meltzer, eds., *Symbolic Interactionism: A Reader in Social Psychology* (Boston: Allyn and Bacon, 1972), pp. 4-22; Arthur Brittain, *Meanings and Situations* (London: Routledge & Kegan Paul, 1973); Norman K. Denzin, "Symbolic Interactionism and Ethnomethodology: A Proposed Synthesis," *American Sociological Review,* 34 (December, 1979):922-934; Manford H. Kuhn, op cit.; Peter Hall, "A Symbolic Interactionist Analysis of Politics," *Sociological Inquiry,* 42 (1972):35-74; Fred Block, "Alternative Sociological Perspectives," *Catalyst* (Winter, 1973):29-42; Dusky Lee Smith, "Symbolic Interactionism: Definitions of the Situation from Becker and Lofland," *Catalyst* (Winter, 1973):62-75; Richard Ropers, "Toward a Phenomenological Sociology," *Catalyst* (Winter, 1973):15-28; Rosabeth M. Kanter, "Symbolic Interactionism and Politics in Systematic Perspective," *Sociological Inquiry,* 42 (1972):77-92; Alvin W. Gouldner, *The Coming Crisis in Western Sociology* (New York: Basic Books, 1970); Leon Shaskolsky, "The Development of Sociological Theory in America: A Sociology of Knowledge Interpretation," in Larry T. and Janice M. Reynolds, eds., *The Sociology of Sociology* (New York: David McKay Co., 1970), pp. 6-30; Joan Huber, "Symbolic Interaction as a Pragmatic Perspective: The Bias of Emergent Theory," *American Sociological* Review, 38 (April, 1973):278-284; Richard Lichtman, "Symbolic Interactionism and Social Reality: Some Marxist Queries," *Berkeley Journal of Sociology,* 15 (1970):75-94.

[15]Each of these is reviewed in reasonable detail by Meltzer, Petras, and Reynolds, op. cit. While there is no difference in the respective visions of the criticisms that have been levied between these authors and the present account, there is substantial difference in the way in which the criticisms are themselves evaluated.

[16]This is the substance of Randall Collin's critique of what he calls interpretive sociology. See his *Conflict Sociology* (New York: Academic Press, 1975), pp. 30-34.

sive importance of the emotions and of the unconscious in human behavior.[17]

4. The methodological demand that the point of view of the actor be incorporated into accounts of behavior, as well as focus on the immediate situation of interaction, on the definitional processes that organize ongoing interaction, and on the emergent character of that organization, act to minimize or deny the facts of social structure and the import of the macro-organizational features of society on behavior. Given this methodological demand and the consequent foci of attention, the perspective is incapable of dealing adequately with the large-scale social organizational features of societies or of the relations among societies.

5. The neglect of social structure—or the facts of class and of power that are inherent in that neglect—constitute an ideological bias in favor of liberal democracy and therefore of the status quo in contemporary American society.

It will be apparent that the version of symbolic interactionism presented in Chapter 3, as well as most of those reviewed in Chapter 4, developed in partial response to some of these criticisms. How well any given version meets these criticisms is open to serious question, as is whether or not various aspects of the critique must be met before symbolic interactionism is viable as theory. Before dealing with such matters, however, it will be useful to look more closely at the criticism which claims an ideological bias in symbolic interactionism.

An ideology is a set of ideas used as a weapon in a political struggle. While there are some who claim that symbolic interactionists wittingly subserve their ideas to political ends,[18] the more responsible argument avoids the *ad hominem* character of that claim to concentrate on the social functions or implications of the idea structure itself.

Philosophically, symbolic interactionism has important roots in pragmatic philosophy. It has roots in German idealism as well, roots that are, above all, represented in its em-

---

[17]Apart from sources cited in footnote 14, on this point see Arnold M. Rose, "Preface," in Arnold M. Rose, ed., *Human Behavior and Social Processes* (Boston: Houghton Mifflin, 1962), pp. vii-xii.

[18]See, for example, Dusty Lee Smith, op. cit.

phasis on the importance of the subjective aspects of human experience and on definitions of the situation. Insofar as the latter limits the reality being studied, it can be argued that objective realities are paid no attention or are at least neglected; and insofar as there is such absence of attention or relative neglect, these objective realities are simply givens. They are taken for granted rather than being made the focus of analysis and in this way tacitly accepted.

The objective realities at issue, of course, largely are the realities of stratification, of the differential distribution of status, wealth, and power in society. Thus, in remarks aimed at Erving Goffman but taken as applicable to symbolic interactionism, Gouldner[19] argues that the theory:

> ... dwells upon the episodic and sees life only as it is lived in a narrow interpersonal circumference, ahistorical and non-institutional, an existence beyond history and society ... which comes alive only in the fluid, transient "encounter."

And that:

> Goffman's rejection of hierarchy often expresses itself as an *avoidance* of social stratification and of the importance of power differences ... thus, it entails an accomodation to existent power arrangements ... (A) dramaturgical model is an accomodation congenial only to those who are willing to accept the basic allocations of existent master institutions ...

Huber[20] comes to the same general view of the ideological consequences of symbolic interactionism, although her starting point is with what she calls the bias of emergent theory located in the framework's origins in pragmatic philosophy. The thesis is that symbolic interactionism along with pragmatism has an epistimology making it reflect the biases of the researcher and the people whose behavior is observed. Pragmatism makes truth dependent on human action. Making truth conditional on the outcome of an event renders knowledge susceptible to social control because the

[19]Gouldner, op. cit., pp. 379-386. Gouldner addresses this criticism specifically to the work of Erving Goffman, but it is not unreasonable to believe that Gouldner would see the criticism as holding for symbolic interactionism generally. Indeed, Meltzer, Petras, and Reynolds, op. cit., p. 101, take the criticisms that Gouldner directs specifically at Goffman and at Howard Becker as the " ... beginnings of a truly systematic, sociological critique of the adequacy of symbolic interactionism as a perspective on human behavior."

[20]Huber, op. cit.

future is subject to the manipulation of those who currently have power. Symbolic interactionism, Huber argues, gives theory no clear place and accords only ambiguous status to formal logic with the consequence that theoretical expectations are not explicated. Truth is expected to come out of interaction and to reflect "what works best" as defined by the emerging consensus of participants in an interaction situation.

> All of these formulations have a status quo bias for, when no theoretical expectations are specified, and when truth is expected to emerge from interaction, then what is taken to be true tends to reflect the distribution of social power among the participants . . . In the absence of theory, the social givens of the researcher and the participants serve as a theoretical framework, giving the research a bias which reflects the unstated assumptions of the researcher, the climate of opinion in the discipline, and the distribution of power in the interactive setting.[21]

There are complexities of a variety of sorts in these claims of an ideological bias in symbolic interactionism, and it is beyond the scope of the present effort to pursue those complexities very far. Indeed, the principal reason for introducing the claims of bias here—apart from the fact that they are part of the literature on symbolic interactionism—is to note that they tie closely to the argument that the framework is incapable of dealing adequately with the facts and the significance of social structure, particularly of social class and power.

For some, more or less orthodox Marxist critics of symbolic interactionism,[22] the truth-value of an assertion is judged in terms of its presumed ideological function. Equating truth with ideological preference means that there is no way to enter the debate over the merits of a theory except in political terms, as a partisan in a political struggle using ideas as weapons; and differences over ideas are resolved only in these terms. Unless one takes a metatheoretical or epistemological stance which defines truth-value independently of ideological function, the game of science as it has

---

[21]Ibid., pp. 276-282. The phrase "all of these formulations" is later indicated as applying to Herbert Blumer, who is viewed as having provided the most sophisticated methodological basis for symbolic interactionism. See p. 279.

[22]Lichtman, op. cit., Shaskolsky, op. cit., and Smith, op. cit., are cases in point.

been understood throughout this work is lost. Gouldner, cited above as an ideological critic of symbolic interaction, nevertheless explicitly recognizes that the cognitive validity of an intellectual system is a separate matter, and argues only that along with their cognitive validity,[23] the ideological sources and consequences of ideas must be judged.

It is useful to realize that weapons may be used "offensively" or "defensively," and that insofar as ideas are indeed weapons, this is necessarily true of ideas. If symbolic interactionism is ideologically a theory supportive of liberal democracy, it will necessarily be "defensive" when that is the nature of the political system and "offensive" when it is not. Thus both the ideological function of a set of ideas and the evaluation of that set of ideas from an ideological point of view may well change with changes in the social scene. In part, this message is implied in Huber's observation that when theoretical premises are unstated they will tend to reflect the biases of the investigators and (for those holding the perspective demanding that the point of view of subjects be incorporated into theorizing) their subjects, and her additional comment that unexplicated theory will reflect the facts of power in the social situation being investigated.

Obviously, these brief comments do not rebut the claim that symbolic interactionism contains an ideological bias. From one standpoint, rebuttal is either useless or impossible. From another standpoint—that which is contained in Chapters 1 and 3 of this volume—the primary response to the claim of ideological bias is the answers to two fundamental and related questions about symbolic interactionism: (1) to what extent is symbolic interactionism taken to be a general framework for the analysis of society or, alternatively, taken to be a partial framework focusing on a (relatively) delimited set of sociological and social psychological problems; and (2) to what extent can social structural concepts be successfully incorporated within symbolic interactionism.

In dealing with these two questions, the discussion necessarily returns to the various symbolic interactionisms, for these differ with respect to their implications for the two

---

[23]Gouldner, op. cit., pp. 12-13.

questions. If, for example, symbolic interactionism is seen as a social-psychological theory addressing problems of socialization and personal organization-disorganization, then the important question becomes whether or not this specialized theory can be articulated reasonably to a sociological orientation that does incorporate structural concepts; the fact that it in itself may not include such concepts is of little significance. If, on the other hand, the claim is that a symbolic interactionism is a general sociological theory, any failure to include attention to status, class, and power as features of social organization as well as any failure to provide for research on and warranted assertions about—say—the relations between nation-states, gives force to the criticism that the theory fails by virtue of its inability to deal with such matters. It gives force, as well, to ideological criticims of the sort made by Gouldner and by Huber.

Blumer's symbolic interactionism, and that of others for which his stands as a reasonable surrogate, does make the claim of generality; it can therefore be faulted for its failure to adequately incorporate structural concepts and concerns. That this version of symbolic interactionism does fail in this way has been argued in prior pages and need not be reargued now.

What of alternative versions of symbolic interactionism? While going beyond the view of symbolic interactionism as a narrow social-psychological perspective, Chapter 3 explicitly eschews the presentation of a general theory. It does not pretend, that is, to be applicable to the full range of problems that may be said to fall within the domain of sociology. Thus, for example, the failure to provide for the relations between nation-states does not in itself vitiate the framework.

But alternative versions of the symbolic interactionism of Chapter 3 and of Chapter 4 as well, are clearly not satisfied to be narrowly-defined, social-psychological theories; they intend some applicability to the conventionally defined sociological domain. To achieve this end, the structural concepts of role theory are incorporated (albeit in varying degree). A symbolic interactionism containing role-theoretic concepts has the means, at least, to deal with many sociological concerns that refer to the relations between or among groups, networks, organizations, and communities.

One is, admittedly, harder put to deal with the relationships among broad social strata—e.g., class conflict—or among nation-states with the conceptual repertoire of a role-theoretic, augmented version of symbolic interactionism. One can, however, recognize the facts of status, class, and power by visualizing them as variables constraining interaction and possible definitions of the situation, as resources used in interactions, and so on. There is, in short, no reason why a symbolic interactionism must fail to incorporate macrosociological, structural variables even if it provides no explanation for the relationships among such variables. Specifically, there is nothing inherent in a symbolic interactionist framework that necessitates either naiveté with reference to, or denial of the facts of differentially distributed power.

It should be reasonably clear that the criticisms levelled against symbolic interactionism, to the effect that its major concepts are imprecise and confused and that it has problems operationalizing its concepts and testing its hypotheses, are differentially valid when measured against the various symbolic interactionisms. The major issue here is whether or not imprecision and problems with operationalization and testing are matters of principle. It is certainly true that to some degree these problems characterize all versions of symbolic interactionism; it could not be otherwise in what is, after all, a developing and changing perspective. It is also certainly true that a symbolic interactionist theory, in the technical sense of theory, has not yet been worked out. Since that is the case, there will of necessity be gaps in the logic connecting many of its ideas, and there will be gaps in the logic connecting these ideas and purported hypotheses. Again, however, the basic issue is whether such gaps are or are not, in principle, part of the framework. If they are, there is no way of dealing satisfactorily with the criticisms, except to say (as Blumer does) that the "real" nature of the empirical social world means that attempts to be precise, to develop a logically integrated theory as the basis for deducing hypotheses, and to test these hypotheses in a rigorous manner are mistaken. If they are not, then the normal activity of science moves us in the direction of greater precision, more adequate logical development, and so on.

The premise of this volume has been that Blumer's rejection of conventional science is not in principle necessary. In varying degree, the remaining formulations of symbolic interactionism reviewed share this premise. To the degree that this volume has successfully accomplished its objectives, it has because of achieving greater precision of concepts, greater logical coherence of ideas, and more reasonable statements of hypotheses. It will not be because these problems have been solved.

The major criticism yet to be reviewed concerns symbolic interactionism's reputed failure to reflect the import of the emotions and of unconscious motivation in human behavior. Closely related is another criticism that can be made: contemporary symbolic interactionism, of whatever variety, neglects the routine and the repetitive in social life. This latter is an especially interesting failing, given that its intellectual sources—from the Scottish Moral Philosophers through Dewey—placed considerable emphasis on habit (on the individual level) and custom (on the collective level). Why this failing is not too difficult to discern. Mead used problem-solving behavior as the paradigm of all human interaction; his evolutionary assumptions led him to see self-consciousness and reflexivity as the essence of the human condition. In a very real sense, he modelled life on the scientific method. Blumer and others, in the pragmatic vein, find the source of action in problematic situations; a "problem," by definition, implies the unavailability of appropriate ready-made patterns of action and calls into play thought processes searching out such patterns. The contemporary emphasis on action as constructed connotes, again at least for many, the deliberative, more-or-less rational aspects of human behavior. All of these lead away from a serious consideration of habit and custom.[24]

They also lead away from a focus on emotions and on

---

[24]A related comment may be made. To say that the individual constructs activity does not deny the possibility (probability) that he or she does so in good part using categories and meanings available in the culture of which he or she is a part. Indeed, it is empirically very likely that most of us most of the time use only such categories and meanings in our construction activity. This implies that, for those of us who share a culture, the construction of activity is likely to proceed using the same sets of meanings. To say this does not argue for the absence of choice, or for a view of action as "culturally determined." It simply denies the appropriateness of conceptualizing constructive activity in terms that overemphasize uniqueness. It is in part an overemphasis on uniqueness which leads to rejecting the possibility of generalization in sociology.

unconscious motivation (in the Freudian sense). Contributing to a neglect of the emotions may have been symbolic interactionism's early tendency to look more to Mead than to Cooley for its intellectual direction. Had the reverse been true, we could well have expected the latter's emphasis on sentiment and affect as compared with the former's emphasis on cognition to result in greater attention to the role of emotion in social life. However this may be, while some interactionists have studied the emotions, and while some work on the self suggests how emotions may be incorporated into symbolic interactionism,[25] the criticism that points out that the framework tends to neglect such is indeed well-taken. The self of the symbolic interactionist has largely been conceptualized in cognitive rather than affective terms; and the framework's concern with significant symbols, meaning, role-taking, communication, and related concepts simply serves to accentuate the point. The framework calls for even less attention to the idea of unconscious motivation.

Having said this, however, leaves open the import of the criticism. Certainly, it would be difficult to deny that the emotions are of significance in social interaction and to deny the existence of phenomena pointed to by the notion of the unconscious. Yet, unless a theory claims to be general enough to be sufficient to the scientific understanding of all aspects of human behavior, the fact that some aspects of behavior are omitted is not absolutely critical to the utility of that theory. With respect to the various symbolic interactionisms, then, again it is those which make the broadest claim of generality that must bear the brunt of this criticism.

The preceding discussion of criticisms of symbolic interactionism and their applicability draws a contrast between the version identified with Blumer and the alternative versions presented in Chapter 3 and 4. That contrast is reasonable. Indeed, given the bases for selection of

[25]See discussion of interactionists' treatment of emotions in Meltzer, Petras, and Reynolds, op. cit., p. 92. Clifford Kirkpatrick formulates an interactionist theory of love in *The Family* (New York: Ronald, 1963), as does Ralph Turner in *Family Interaction* (New York: Wiley, 1970). See also the suggestion in Stryker, "Identity Salience and Role Performance," op. cit., that the self be viewed as having cathectic and conative modalities as well as congnitive.

work to be covered in this volume, that contrast is inevitable. But, as the concluding note in Chapter 4 asserts, there are differences as well as similarities among the set of alternative (to Blumer's) symbolic interactionisms. McCall is less structural, and so closer to Blumer, than is Turner, who is less structural in orientation than any of the remaining versions. Burke is more oriented to rigorous measurement procedures than are the rest, although Weinstein is close in this respect and I find myself quite comfortable with Burke's emphases.[26] Precision of conceptualization is clearly an important intent in my own work and that of Burke, with the others more in sympathy with a "sensitizing concept" orientation. All seek to formulate and to test hypotheses, but Turner is much more inductive in his procedure than are the others, who tend more toward working deductively from abstract theory to hypotheses. Weinstein is more eclectic in his theorizing than are the rest, with McCall next, and therefore perhaps more likely to see the focus of symbolic interactionism per se in relatively narrow terms. It may be that Weinstein's concepts of trace and template provide a way for reintroducing habit and even the unconscious into interactionist theorizing, and it may be that Turner's concept of the impulsive self provides a way of thinking about the role of emotion in interaction; each of the others introduce distinctive concepts that perhaps give their formulations advantages in other respects.

That these differences exist is neither surprising nor disheartening. From the perspective of the philosophic context from which symbolic interactionism emerged, thought, categories, and knowledge are not "of themselves" but develop in terms of and are shaped by the problems one is faced with and sets out to solve. As intellectual issues shift, then, we ought expect symbolic interactionism to change in its emphases, to incorporate new concepts, and to adopt new research tactics. Theory, at its best, is not static.

In Conclusion

It is obvious that the variety of criticisms that have been and can be made of symbolic interactionism in any of its versions, are not taken here to be damning. If they were,

---

[26]Indeed, we are collaborators in ongoing research as well as colleagues.

there would have been little point—outside of possible historical interest—in writing this volume. To assert that the criticisms are not damning is not, however, to dismiss them or to assert that they are unimportant. Rather, the assertion means that those who work in the symbolic interactionist vein need continuously to strive for greater precision of concepts and more reasonable research procedures. They must also strive to work out better the logic of the relationship between social structure and individual behavior, between macro- and micro-social processes. To the degree that these directions are taken, symbolic interactionism will remain a viable theoretical alternative in sociology. The hope is that the present effort has contributed to this end.

Index